D0445029

The Politically Correct Guide to

American History

The Politically Correct Guide to

American History

Edward P. Moser

Crown Publishers, Inc. • *New York*

To Maryanne, for her steadfast support,
and Donna, for her reading lessons

Published by Crown Publishers, Inc., 201 East 50th Street, New York,
New York 10022. Member of the Crown Publishing Group.

Random House, Inc. New York, Toronto, London, Sydney, Auckland

Crown and colophon are trademarks of Crown Publishers, Inc.

Manufactured in the United States of America

LIBRARY OF CONGRESS CATALOGING-IN-PUBLICATION DATA
IS AVAILABLE UPON REQUEST.

ISBN 0-517-70410-2

10 9 8 7 6 5 4 3 2 1

First Edition

Contents

Acknowledgments

Thanks is gratefully expressed to the long-term members of the "mailing list." And to the O'Briens and Linda for the software, Mike for the business advice, Nancy for the walks, and Gam and TL for the editorial advice. Also J&R for the time, T&J for the softball.

I'd like to thank Carol Taylor, and the rest of the editing and production folks at Crown Publishers, for their close attention to detail. Especially to Jim for the final scrubbing. Also to Paul Bachem for the jacket illustration.

Special thanks to Joe Ajlouny for placing the book.

Further, to selfless instructors Matthew LeStrange and Fr. John Shelley, for instilling a love of history.

Appreciation to such favorites as: Russell Baker, Dave Barry, Art Buchwald, Joseph Conrad, Norman Lear, Monty Python, Vladimir Nabokov, P. J. O'Rourke, H. L. Mencken, S. J. Perelman (any author with two initial initials), Hunter Thompson, Voltaire, Tom Wolfe, and Dublin's Dean Swift.

E pluribus unum.
(Out of one, many.)

Introduction

The Politically Correct Guide to American History is a primer on the past as it should be taught in schools. It reflects proposed new national standards for teaching herstory. Some chapters retell for modern tastes actual events like Thomas Jefferson's sexual harassment of Sally Hemings and the drowning of defenseless herbs during the "Boston Tea Party." Other chapters refashion legendary tales like the woodland devastation wreaked by lumber-jane Paula Bunyan. Alternative, inoffensive excerpts from the Bill of Rights and the Declaration of Independence are provided. A section on the Lincoln presidency exposes its harsh intolerance of regional diversity, as expressed by its refusal to grant Union army commissions to Confederate officers. Misunderstood elements of society—the vertically unendowed, private militias, insect companions, and prison residents—who have been banished from the mainstream of American life are finally given their due.

This document focuses on the founding and development of the Euro-American state, from the voyage of the pirate Christopher Columbus through the presidency of the equestrian exploiter Teddy Roosevelt. As the present is indelibly linked to the past, the narrative at times oddly echoes our current age. The discerning reader will find similarities between the text and contemporary concerns including the O. J. Simpson trial, health and safety laws, and assorted (and sordid) political scandals.

The Politically Correct Guide to American History deconstructs and redesigns the story of the United States to conform to a rapidly changing, postmodern, multicultural world. No longer can accounts of this nation's past focus on the militaristic and scentist misdeeds of deceased myn of off-color at the expense of excluded unisex, hermaphroditic, and Antarctic-American communities, among other victimized groups.

Sensitive readers are forewarned they may be disturbed by some of the accounts and descriptions contained herein. Each book purchaser, therefore, is asked to sign the following prereading agreement, which absolves the author of legal liability for mental or physical disabilities resulting from examination of the text:

I hereby certify that the writer, or the companies supplying him with pen and ink to construct this document, shall not be held responsible for any psychological trauma, medical conditions, or toxic chemicals acquired from turning the pages of The Politically Correct Guide to American History.

Signed,

_____

*I*n 1787 the Founding Parents Drew Up the Constitution

In 1787 D.C.E. (During the Current Era), the Founding Parents gathered in Philadelphia, the City of Sibling Affection, to devise new rules for running Turtle Island, the Indigenous Persons' name for America. The Constitutional Convention was a "meeting of the demigoddesses" that included some of the most prominent Anglo-Saxon males in the country. Revolutionary general George Washington presided over the assembly with lips sternly and habitually pursed from his dentural deprivation. As in any exclusively male enterprise, the delegates spent much of their time publicly scratching their private parts, expelling oral fluids (spittoons were thoughtfully placed in every chamber), and getting lost on their way to the convention out of an obstinate refusal to ask for directions.

The Founding Parents were lifestyle bigots who frowned on out-of-wedlock births. However, the delegates' wearing of powdered wigs, ruffled lace shirts, silk stockings, and high-heeled shoes evidenced a healthy attitude toward cross-dressing. Many of the Founders were Masons, a conspiratorial society of tassel-hatted retirees lusting to establish a New World Order. On the subject of religion, many Founders were deists, which meant they believed in God but didn't regularly go to church, which is the reverse of many present-day politicians.

Benny* Franklin, at 81 years the most chronologically prominent delegate, was author of *Fiscally Challenged Richard's Almanac* and inventor of the bifocal lens for the visually impoverished. Over two hundred years after his unregulated electrical experiments with kite and key, Franklin's nation is riddled with high-powered transmission lines and associated high cancer rates. On voyages to Europe, Franklin the scientist had discovered the warm-water Gulf Stream, which was early evidence of the green-

* The current custom is to refer to political leaders informally by their first name, as in Vice President Al Gore and Libyan statesman Muammar "Mo" Gadhafi.

house effect. Despite his advanced years, Franklin received no government pension or medical benefits and wasn't a member of any powerful elderly citizens' lobby. He cruelly believed that ever-growing subsidies to the retired would bankrupt his nation and impoverish his grandchildren.

Delegates Al Hamilton and Tommy Jefferson engaged in a running dispute over the role of government. Hamilton supported a strong federal government with broad authority to tax and spend. Jefferson supported states' rights and tough restrictions on taxes and spending. Hamilton is traditionally described as the first Republican, and Jefferson the first Democrat, but it is obvious the reverse is true. The otherwise unforgivable absence of female delegates denied the notorious Jefferson the opportunity of committing additional acts of gender harassment. (Few "conventioneers" since have been so celibate.) As the first treasury secretary, Hamilton went on to balance the budget by taxing almost 0.14 percent of people's incomes, pushing "Tax Freedom Day" all the way to January 5. In a fatal duel with Aaron Burr, Hamilton was shot because the ownership of handgun ammunition was legal.

The Constitutional Convention met in the sweltering summer of an era that lacked air-conditioning, fortunately, for the freon gas used to cool air contributes to ozone depletion. Gathering in closed rooms under near-tropical conditions, the delegates rejected scentism and breathed the revolutionary notion that the corporeal fragrance of a Georgian is no different than the smell of a Rhode Islander. Still, the convention's shuttered, closely guarded conferences stemmed from the belief of two-faced delegates, touting "freedom of the press," that an irresponsible, sensation-seeking media would publish any news leaks. The convention had no television cameras, which hardly mattered because speakers gave the kind of lofty philosophical declarations that would have drawn a tiny ratings share and brought about immediate cancellation.

Strangely enough, the delegates asked Jimmy Madison to write the Constitution on principle and forgo basing it on opinion polls and focus groups pegged to passing voter concerns. Whenever Madison wearied of writing, he chilled out by taking a constitutional around Philadelphia. His live-in partner, "Dolley" Payne Madison, who had disgraced herself by accepting a sexist, patronizing nickname, would later cheerfully manage the Madison administration's social calendar instead of demanding an influential seat in cabinet discussions.

The Payne-Madisons were in office during the so-called War of 1812, which broke out after the failed diplomacy of the 1812 Peace Overture. During the war, British invaders burned down the White House, even though Pennsylvania Avenue had been closed to unauthorized personnel. The conflict spawned the national anthem, penned by Francis Scott Key while watching an English ship bombard Baltimore's Harborplace. The often-repeated song is played at the start of televised baseball games to make what follows less tedious. Jimmy Madison was the protégé of Jimmy Monroe, who as president formulated the "Monroe Doctrine," by which a handsome, charismatic president could have a discreet affair with a blond Hollywood starlet.

The most important part of the Constitution is its "Bill

of Lefts."* The Bill of Lefts guarantees basic liberties such as freedom of the press and freedom of alternative religions like the 700 Club. These first amendments to the Constitution, as revised for modern sensibilities, include the following:

- *No person can be accused of a crime unless there is compelling evidence presented to a grand jury, except in cases where a Supreme Court justice or a president is charged, on the basis of hearsay, with sexual harassment accounts that allegedly occurred a decade or more ago, in which case the accused shall be found guilty by public opinion and through the character assassination of an unmerciful press.*

- *A well-regulated militia being necessary to maintain a free country, members of a militia or terrorist group caught blowing up buildings shall be free to exercise a legal defense blaming their acts on unwitting complicity, uncontrollable emotions, the overwrought rhetoric of political pundits, assorted war-related ailments or syndromes, or other facile excuses.*

- *No humyn person shall be subject to "double jeopardy" unless he or she willingly agrees to appear on a nationwide game show.*

- *The right to bear arms shall not be infringed, except for waiting periods, for certain types of rifles and pistols, for various ammunitions, and for crime-plagued cities that ban*

---

* Or Bill of Rights, or Hillary of Rights. "Lefts" is an acceptable alternative term for rights, a term which favors the right-handed persons who have dominated society from time immemorial.

all guns owned by law-abiding citizens and under-siege shopkeepers.

- The accused shall enjoy an impartial jury of the district in which the crime was committed—except in cases presuming racial prejudice, whereby the trial shall be moved to another district on the presumption that all the local jurors are prejudiced. To assure the absence of racism, the jury members shall be selected on the basis of race.

- Congress shall make no law abridging freedom of speech, except for V chips, Internet guidelines, and music warning labels. Congress shall make no law in respect to the establishment of a religion, except for private school vouchers, nor any law restricting the free exercise of religion, except for school prayer.

- No law shall infringe upon the freedom of the press to libel. When a newspaper smears someone, it shall ignore its error, or admit it many editions later on the bottom of page 57.

- No person shall be held answerable to a crime unless indicted, except during citywide curfews, in which case the rights of every person under a certain age to free assembly shall be void and forfeit.

- In all criminal prosecutions, the accused shall enjoy the right to a speedy trial, except where lawyers benefit from the higher legal fees of a prolonged trial, or where the presiding judge fears the slightest departure from established procedure will result in a mistrial, or worse, an appeal, forcing a repeat of the whole drawn-out process.

- *Any affluent person convicted of a serious crime shall serve only a limited sentence in a "country club" prison.*

- *Private property shall not be taken for public use without just compensation, except in all cases—without reservation—involving Native Americans, or for environmental laws that regulate privately owned land. The Constitution's allocation of certain limited rights to the government shall include all other rights previously retained by the people.*

- *The right of persons to be secure in their homes against unreasonable search and seizure shall not be violated, unless the federal agents outside the building are too tired to wait around any longer.*

- *The right of preadults* (children and adolescents) to be secure in their persons, rooms, toys, papers, and other effects against unreasonable searches and seizures by parents shall not be violated, even when suspected of illicit narcotic possession or use within the home. No drug-sniffing animal companion nor chemically based drug test shall be permitted on the person or property of the preadults, nor may a "drug-free zone" be declared within the house.*

- *Involuntary servitude in the United States shall not exist, except for contributors to deficit reduction (taxpayers).*

- *Those powers not delegated to the United Nations by the Constitution are reserved for the United States.*

---

* "Preadult," a word that implies full legal lefts (rights), is the preferred term for child or infant.

Jimmy Madison wrote his Constitution in a highly learned style that wrongly presumes the value of standards in education and defames the earthier, more spontaneous speech of semiliterate common people. To correct his error, the Constitution can be reprinted in "dumbed-down," Anglo-Saxon English stripped of elitist words derived from Latin and French. The preamble to the Constitution is shown below in both its original elitist and revised, "populist" style:

Latin-French Elitist	Anglo-Saxon Populist
We, the people of the United States, in order to form a more perfect Union,	*We, the folks of the Big Bailiwicks Which Stand Together, so that to make a more wholesome Togetherness,*
establish justice, insure domestic tranquillity, provide for the common defense,	*call into being fairness, make happen stillness at home, ready a warrior's shield for all,*
promote the general welfare, and secure the blessings of liberty	*foster a sweeping well-being, and get the bounty of freedom*
to ourselves and our posterity, do ordain and establish	*to ourselves and our children's children, do pick and make stand*
this Constitution for the United States of America.	*this Drawing Up Together for the Big Bailiwicks Which Stand Together of the Land named after the man from the Land that looks like a kicking foot.*

The Founding Mothers matriotically strove to ease regional conflicts in the new nation. Southerners and Northerners were already making fun of the way each other talked, and concern over such accent discrimination prompted the Founders to encourage settlement, through land surveys and property grants, of the Midwest: They figured settlers there would speak in flat, neutral tones that wouldn't offend anyone. Further, they fought geographic discrimination by guaranteeing representation for citizens of each major territorial block, or state. However, this artifice resulted in some oddly shaped voting districts, like the electoral map of Maryland's U.S. Senate district below:

The illustration shows that, in the case of Maryland, clever "redistricting" made certain that someone of Maryland-American heritage would be elected.

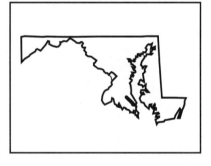

To placate the South, the Founders agreed to put the nation's capital in the new city of Washington, D.C., which French architect Pierre L'Preadult (Pierre L'Enfant) designed. L'Preadult built the town on wetlands that were breeding grounds for aquatic birds and mosquitoes before their senseless draining for phallocentric constructions like the Washington Monument. The architect garlanded his creation with broad boulevards, probably to enable the easy movement of troops intent on crushing the inevitable popular insurrections, as well as for responding to drive-by shootings and mayoral drug busts.

As evidenced by the Lincoln and Jefferson memorials, the city grew into a veritable shrine to DWEMs, or dead white European males—as opposed to dead white Indonesian males—whose greedy countenances smirk from the front of their respective almighty dollar denominations. Another Washington landmark is the jingoistic Vietnam Memorial, which, while faithfully listing the name of every slain American, ignores the countless foreign soldiers who selflessly gave their lives to deter Yankee aggression.

Some Founding Parents who desired a strong central government wanted to make Martha Dandridge* Washington the queen, but Martha demurred, so the convention settled for a powerful president and First Partner. The date for the president's inauguration was set for March, and later moved back to January to allow sufficient time for the State of the Union speech.

As the new government of President George Dandridge Washington had only three departments—Treasury, State, and War—few would have noticed a federal shutdown. The budget-conscious urged privatizing the War Department by hiring the Vatican's Swiss Guards as part-time employees. The new Treasury Department printed currency with militaristic slogans like "Don't Tread on Me" instead of more inclusive expressions like "Practice

---

* Dandridge was the pre–domestic incarceration name, or premarital "maiden name," of Martha Dandridge Washington, George Washington's Significant Other. Nongenderist males may adopt as their middle names the "maiden name" of their spouse.

Random Acts of Kindness." The first government also had an attorney general, a post for which the president usually picks his most trusted confidant, unless that person is writing a "kiss-and-tell" book about their relationship.

The Constitutional Convention established ground rules for the legislative branch, such as an elected House of Representatives run by a Speaker, so called because he was expected to talk at great length, volume, and glibness about the most important concerns of the day, such as himself. The controlling party in the Senate is run by a majority leader, and the out-of-power party by a nonmajoritarian leader. The Constitution forbids members of Congress from taking bribes, but it is mum about overseas junkets, lavish pensions, and lucrative book deals.

Reflecting its ageist philosophy, the document sets minimum age requirements for congresspersons and the president, but not the latter's staff. In an ultranationalist passage, it forbids noncitizens and visiting foreign tourists from holding government office. Voting is officially called "suffrage" to describe the ballot-booth anguish of facing a "Hobson's choice" of woeful candidates.

For a long time Congress exempted itself from laws, such as noise abatement, which it passed for the rest of the country. Consumer protection laws against false advertising were not applied to candidates' campaign commercials. To judge from the partisan invective that has characterized Congress, hate speech laws have never pertained. After-the-fact or *ex post facto* laws were forbidden, except for retroactive tax hikes that collect the already-spent wages of previous years.

The Constitution is silent on term limits: The courts decide what jail sentences to impose on convicted politicians. As for restrictions on the number of congressional terms a member can serve, the party out of power is usually for them, and the party in power opposed. Such restrictions might be harmful because they would strengthen the influence of permanent Washington interests like lobbies, which are largely composed of retired members of Congress.

The original Constitution limited the right to vote to property owners, which sadly is not the case today, considering the federal government is the country's largest property owner. Under the prior, superior scheme, Washington's permanent bureaucracies could continually reappoint themselves without having to worry about nuisances such as elections and referenda.

*P*resident George Washington, the Parent of Our Country, Meets the Press

George Washington, the Founding Parent of our country, met only once with newspaper reporters before abruptly canceling a series of planned future conferences. This chapter contains the press conference's transcript. Certain terms and topics have been altered to avoid offending postmodern readers.

REPORTER: Mr. President, an unnamed, unattributed source within your administration claims you never actually murdered a cherry tree. Is the allegation true? And if you did kill the tree, doesn't it indicate a callousness toward defenseless plant species?

WASHINGTON: The story of my chopping down, murdering as you say, my biological father's cherry tree was purely allegorical. The part where I admitted the deed to my dad illustrates my basic honesty, but was not intended as a literal version of events. Let me emphasize the tale was disseminated by political aides without my knowledge. I acknowledge my environmental insensitivity although, as I said, the deed as reported did not literally occur. Let me add the cherry tree incident occurred over fifty years ago, when attitudes toward the care of the earth were very different.

REPORTER: What's your comment on the revelation that, during the French and Indigenous Persons Conflict, you fought on the side of our colonial oppressors the British?

WASHINGTON: But you're referring to alleged behavior from over four decades in the past!

REPORTER: You deny the allegation?

WASHINGTON (stammering): I, I don't, I, uh, ah . . .

REPORTER: Wasn't it a conflict of interest, during the American Revolution, for you to command armed forces fighting the British, when some time before you were on

Britain's payroll? How does your action, sir, differ from what Benedict Arnold did?

WASHINGTON: It's true that in 1754, some forty years ago, I accompanied a British general on an ill-fated incursion against the French and their Native American allies.

REPORTER: Have you experienced remorse about the invasion?

WASHINGTON: It was obviously a judgment error on my part to take up arms against the Indigenous Persons, who were only seeking to defend their ancestral homes from Anglo-American aggression.

REPORTER: What about the conflict of interest?

WASHINGTON: In hindsight, at the time of assuming control of the Revolutionary army, I should have given the Continental Congress detailed records of my financial transactions with the Brits.

REPORTER: Sir, could you explain another story, about your supposed throwing of a coin across the Potomac? At some points the river is nearly two hundred meters across, an impossible distance for the strongest hurler. What was the breadth of the river where you performed this alleged feat?

WASHINGTON: Frankly, I don't recall the details of the matter.

REPORTER: Is the basic thrust of the story true? Or was the coin tossing "purely allegorical"?

WASHINGTON: I've been meaning to make a full accounting of this event, and I will make good on my intent in due course. The coin throwing, like the cherry tree killing, took place many years ago, which accounts for the haziness of my memory. But again, I will soon release all pertinent facts concerning this critical subject.

REPORTER: Mr. President, the actual length of your toss is only half the issue. An innocent fish could have swallowed an underthrown coin that fell beneath the waves.

WASHINGTON: Many a night that thought has kept me awake. All I can say is I haven't thrown so much as a pebble into a body of water since. And I urge every youngster to shun skipping flattened rocks across the surface of our nation's water resources. . . . You know, back in the Revolution, when I ferried those troops across the icy Delaware, I made sure our equipment was securely lashed, lest anything harmful to marine life be inadvertently knocked overboard.

REPORTER: Mr. First Partner, concerning the media firestorm over your oath of office: If you were inaugurated again, would—

WASHINGTON: —I would swear on a Hindu Veda. Placing my hand on a Bible was in no way meant to exclude or demean persons of nontraditional faith.

REPORTER: Would you comment on persistent reports of your womynizing?

WASHINGTON: Well, the nerve—

REPORTER: I refer, Mr. President, to the rumors, circulating in many cities, that "Washington slept here."

WASHINGTON: Do you imply—

REPORTER: —Do you deny that in your extensive travels as president and general you've bedded down in hundreds of taverns offering cheap, even tawdry, overnight accommodations? Do you deny that all sexes might be attracted to you, a powerful, fiscally advantaged* politician, in such an intimate setting? And what is Martha's take on these charges?

WASHINGTON: Leave my domestic incarceration partner out of it!

REPORTER: To put it plainly, sir: Are you "first in the hearts of your countrywomyn"?

WASHINGTON: Have the members of the press no sense of damaged self-esteem?†

REPORTER: Is that a denial?

WASHINGTON: My denial is categorical.

REPORTER: What does "categorical" mean?

WASHINGTON: No one knows. That's why I use the term: It gives me "plausible deniability."

REPORTER: Mr. President, regarding another conflict of

---

* Rich. The terms "rich" and "poor" can foster class conflict and fuel feelings of inadequacy among the remuneratively challenged.
† Shame.

interest flap . . . Is your administration run by a "Virginia Mafia"? Many note your ties to James Monroe, Patrick Henry, Jeffer—

WASHINGTON: —But all these are financially endowed, melanin-deprived, male humyns of merit!

REPORTER: But wouldn't the property value of their plantations benefit from the planned placement of the nation's new capital on the border of their state? And isn't it a bit presumptuous, sir, to name the new capital after yourself?

WASHINGTON: Next question!

REPORTER: What's your view of draining the marshes—which some believe are carriers of disease—on which the new capital will be built?

WASHINGTON: I worry about the net loss of wetlands that would result. That drainage notion should be put out to Pasteur.

REPORTER: A more mundane matter, sir: For years, you've claimed to wear wooden teeth, and have obtained some sympathy from the denturally disadvantaged for your disability. But aren't your teeth actually made of lead?

WASHINGTON: I cannot make a misstatement.* The truth is my artificial teeth were once wooden. But all the criticism over the cherry tree massacre made me realize it's wrong to put slain vegetable matter in one's mouth. Personally, I

---

* "I cannot tell a lie."

would make an exception for salads, but that's for each individual to decide. Long ago, I removed my wooden teeth and, after giving the plant carcass a decent burial, replaced them with ones of lead.

REPORTER: You're not an adherent, sir, of the theory that lead in the bloodstream is a risk to humyn health?

WASHINGTON: I'd rather put my own life in peril than risk the possible slaughter of another innocent plant. Besides, I only use the teeth when I eat, so I think the ill health effects are minimal.

REPORTER: Sir, is your powdered wig purely for show, or does it cloak your tonsural deprivation?*

WASHINGTON: I see someone in the back has a question.

REPORTER: Turning to foreign relations, Mr. President, many Americans still wonder about the heavily foreign staff you assembled during the Revolution. I'm referring to the Polish officer Casimir Pulaski, your notorious Germanic disciplinarian Baron "von"† Steuben, and the Frenchperson Lafayette. Didn't these foreign lobbyists have an unsavory, excessive influence over our cause?

WASHINGTON: I'm not one to cower behind the standards of the past, but in 1776 there were no rules governing interaction with foreign officials.

REPORTER: What about the autocratic implications of these

---

* Baldness.
† "Von," a term indicating aristocratic ancestry, should be used sparingly by egalitarian nonelitists.

dangerous liaisons? Most of the foreigners, such as the Marquis de Lafayette, were nobles, and now you surround yourself with homegrown aristocrats like Thomas Jefferson. Do your personal contacts, sir, suggest your ultimate aim is to be king?

WASHINGTON: I'm bringing the press conference to a close. My gums are aching from all this talk; I really must go.

(Washington storms out. He is overheard muttering the following:) Why did I ever take this thankless job? Madison's a bright fellow, but his Constitution neglected to place checks and balances on the media. Of course I was elected president by a unanimous vote: Why would any sensible person run for this office, given all the guff one must endure?

A Politically Corrected Columbus

A melanin-deprived person known to herstory as Christopher Columbus was born in Genoa, Italy, in 1451 D.C.E. (During the Current Era). The infant was named after Saint Christopher, the so-called "patron saint" of travelers. The choice of this name by Ms. and Mr. Columbus—although suggesting a belief in outmoded belief constructs—proved prophetic.

Columbus's father was a wool weaver—that is, a shameless expropriator of the body hair of a defenseless vegetarian animal, the sheep. Columbus's mother, like most womyn of the time, was coerced into early child-rearing by social pressure and the lack of widely available, easily affordable contraceptives.

Frustrated by his antiquated nuclear family, the young Columbus engaged in a typical act of adolescent rebellion, and took to the sea at age nineteen. Sadly, this career decision betrayed a shocking disregard for biological diversity. After all, the vessels of the time were built out of living pines brutally ripped from the earth by callous, ax-wielding tree murderers.

In his first voyage, Columbus sailed with a band of mercenaries seeking to conquer a patriotic, emerging-nation* group known as the Barbary pirates. Happily, Columbus's Eurocentric fleet was destroyed in battle off the coast of Portugal. Wounded and flung overboard, Columbus was saved from drowning when a floating piece of reworked tree carcass—an oar—just happened to drift his way.

Despite this setback, Columbus stubbornly stuck to his seafaring dream. A success-driven yuppie, he became obsessed with a fantasy of shipping off to distant realms to search for silver and gold. His crass materialism was reinforced by a firm conviction that the earth was round, not the imperfectly shaped oval we now know it to be.

After his shipwreck, Columbus remained for several years in Portugal, where he grew familiar with the natives' bar-

---

* Third-world country.

barous customs. Every autumn, hordes of tree-slaughtering woodsmyn cut down whole forests to generate timber for ships. The blood of the slain wood products was turned into resin for making the ships watertight. Other Portuguese earned a livelihood by stripping cork trees of their very marrow, and stuffing the *once-living tissue* into the necks of bottles. Still other natives made wine to fill the bottles by stomping on thousands of defenseless grapes with their bare, stinking feet!

During his stay, Columbus tried persuading the local king to finance his dream of an overseas journey. But Portugal's ruler refused, as he already had an empire in Africa, where the Egyptians had invented European science thousands of years earlier. Rebuffed by the cork-killing, grape-stomping Portuguese, the would-be explorer traveled to Spain to seek another sponsor. Fortunately for Columbus, the Spanish monarchy of that time was progressive on issues of gender. An assertive, intelligent womyn—Queen Isabella—sat atop the country's throne, and looked kindly on Columbus's scheme.

Isabella's sexual partner—King Ferdinand—was an enlightened humyn person who practiced full equality in his chief domestic arrangement, and even empowered his spouse to develop Spain's streamlined, cost-effective system of nationalized health care. Ferdinand was proud his Significant Other had forged an independent career path, and grateful at the second income she brought home to help feed their offspring, whom he helped raise by taking "family leave" from the court.

While Isabella was sympathetic to Columbus, she won-

dered if the adventurer had the maritime experience for the
arduous voyage he proposed. Her doubts were put to rest
by her counselor, who said, "Don't fret, Izzy—that
Columbus fellow is the Genoan article." So Isabella granted
Columbus a fleet of ships and a crew. She funded the trip by
selling the crown jewels and investing the cash in Spain's
bullish *toro,* or cattle futures market, instantly earning
through insider trading a thousand-percent profit.

Despite the involvement of the queen, the expedition's
personnel policy was alarmingly sexist. As Spain did not
permit womyn to serve in its armed forces or merchant
marine, every member of the ninety-person crew was
male. The gender discrimination occurred despite physical
characteristics that make she-people superior sailpersons.
For example, because womyn have more body fat than
men, they are better swimmers, and are more suited to surviving long voyages on nothing but hardtack and tainted
water.

According to the chauvinist custom of the day,
Columbus patronizingly gave female names to each of his
ships. The *Niña,* the *Pinta,* and the *Santa Maria* all had the
Spanish feminine ending "a." The term *Niña* (The Girl)
was belittling in tone. The term for the flagship, *Santa
Maria* (Holy Mary), constituted a clear violation of sepa-
ration between church and state. The term *Pinta* (Painted
Lady) honored the cosmetic products that make womyn
slaves to their appearance.

In August (Julian calendar) of 1492 (D.C.E.), Columbus
left port, after a lawsuit by a civil liberties group failed to
block a public, nonsectarian prayer for the sailors' safe

return. The all-male crew passed by Gibraltar, once called the Pillars of Hercules—whose symbolic representation of naked masculine power needs no explanation. (Because the actual name of Columbus, Cristóbal Colón, is itself a blatant display of naked masculine power, the name "Columbus" is preferred.)

After sailing into the Atlantic, the fleet paused to take on provisions at the Canary Islands, whose naming after a tropical bird was a welcome and unusual example of nonspeciesism by a culture that more typically named a newly discovered place after a dead white nobleman. Then the band of *conquistadores* headed west into uncharted seas.

Despite its inherent sexism, Columbus's fleet showed signs of being environmentally sensitive and socially aware. Because their sails were driven by sun-generated wind, the *Niña,* the *Pinta,* and the *Santa Maria* were in effect solar-powered craft. And as the ships were newly invented caravels that could sail against the wind, Columbus dispensed with the then-customary deck of oar-pulling galley slaves.

Because refrigeration was unknown, the fleet generated no ozone-depleting chemicals. However, the same lack of coolants, combined with the absence of Rubbermaid containers and Ziploc bags, did lead to minor annoyances like scurvy. The inability to preserve food also caused near-starvation among the crew. More importantly, however, the sailpersons had no unsightly plastic trash to toss overboard.

By early October, after two months of travel, whispers of

mutiny were heard among Columbus's famished, bacteria-hosting* crew. The sailpersons were upset at being lost at sea. Those unhappy with their jobs weren't allowed to apply for early retirement. The stressed-out sailpeople could not even look forward to an October 12 holiday that today we take for granted. Moreover, the fleet's lack of a diversity-awareness counselor sparked cross-cultural misunderstandings. The crew sometimes misinterpreted the gestures of Columbus—an Italian who "spoke with his hands"—as commands to change direction, and as a result strayed off course.

Captain Columbus possessed few means of soothing his restive crew. The Spanish navy of the fifteenth century had no formal mechanism for mediating worker-management disputes. Because the right to strike was not widely recognized, any sailor caught in a labor slowdown was forced to "transit the sliver of tree carcass" (walk the plank), or be hung by "the meter-arm" (the yardarm†). Columbus finally bribed his wage slaves into obedience by promising a large reward for the first person to sight land.

After all hope seemed lost, the fleet came across signs it was near a coastal ecosystem. Bunches of deceased leaves and chunks of demised driftwood floated past. Species of water fowl, some enjoying a final moment of peace before their slaughter by rubber-booted, shotgun-toting settlers,

---

* Disease-ridden. "Disease" carries a negative connotation toward certain epidemic-bearing microscopic species.

† This document strictly follows the metric system of weights and measures, as opposed to the English system based on the body parts—for example, "feet"—of deceased, melanin-deficient monarchs.

flew overhead. Finally, on October 12, the expedition reached landfall.

The landing party was an odd assortment of socially regressive elements. The priests accompanying the expedition excluded wompeople from their ranks. In fact, womyn were not permitted to serve as altar girls, or to stand up at Mass and strum songs of global solidarity on folk guitar.

The soldiers in the landing party also barred from their profession all womyn—not to mention pacifists. Imperial Spain had no equivalent of a naval WAVE organization that might have given matriotic womyn a socially acceptable means of serving their country. A double whammy of a double standard existed for matriotic womyn of diverse gender orientation seeking to enlist, as there was no "Don't Ask, Don't Tell" recruitment option.

Soon after coming ashore, Columbus and his men encountered Indigenous Persons. The most significant "discovery" of the voyage was that the inhabitants lived in complete harmony with Nature. Subsisting on a low-caloric, low-cholesterol diet of roots, berries, and veggies, few natives experimented with self-defeating fad diets. Freed from the straitjacket of modern medicine and sanitation, most died before age thirty, which prevented the societal disruptions caused by population growth. Future battles with the Europeans would reduce their numbers even more, although illnesses transmitted from the new arrivals were the largest cause of the natives' decline. In 1500 D.C.E., there were no vaccines for deadly diseases like vertically challenged pox (smallpox), which today is on the verge of eradication, unless it is placed on the Endangered Species List, as many have urged.

Many Indigenous Peoples were humyn sacrifice enthusiasts, and thrilled to a time-honored pastime with clear benefits for demographic limitation. Although natives often engaged in bloody, intertribal conflict resolutions, or wars, they made practical use of their slain opponents' body parts. Scalps of the vanquished were brandished about in drunken, postdispute ceremonies of peace.

After interfacing with the Indigenous Peoples, Columbus spent the balance of the year cruising around the "West Indies." Because he encountered several tropical storms, the adventurer may have started the genderphobic tradition, now discarded, of naming himmicanes (hurricanes) exclusively after womyn. For the return voyage, the explorer took back many samples of native plant and animal life, without first obtaining the legal consent of these nonhumyn species.

Columbus has been called the "discoverer" of the "New World," but many preceded him to Turtle Island, the preferred, Native Persons' term for "America." The Egyptians, the race of ebony warriors who dominated the ancient world, probably sailed to Turtle Island on boats fashioned from recycled papyrus. The Vikings, a pale-haired race of noncolor, also preceded Columbus. In naming Turtle Island "Vinland" (Wine Land), these water-borne warriors betrayed the same fetish for grape-stomping cruelty as the Portuguese. Thousands of years before, soon-to-be Indigenous Persons had crossed from Siberia to Turtle

Island over a natural land bridge resulting from a drop in ocean levels relating to the growth of the polar ice caps, a sign of "global cooling" induced by Neanderthal Man's under-supervised campfires, whose airborne particles reflected warming sunlight back into outer space.

After his herstoric voyage, Columbus returned to the "New World" three more times, but he never received a frequent traveler discount coupon, nor did he find any silver or gold. The famed sailperson died penniless, as his society—which declined to place an exorbitant tax on the younger generation to pay for the leisure of its elders—lacked a secure, fully solvent system of retirement compensation.

Farmer Stone Meets the Victimized Devil and Daniel Webster

Farmer Stone's name reflected the rocky, fertile-averse condition of his New Hampshire property. In the flinty soil of the Granite State, Stone had disappointing harvests. As a result, he had inferior feed for his incarcerated farm animals. As a consequence, he could burglarize just a few ovaries a week from the hens clucking mournfully behind the chicken-wire fence of their poultry prison.

While sitting on a stool to sexually harass his she-goat's shrunken udders, he glanced morosely at the almost empty pail of lactal liquid. Hanging his head, he moaned, "I'd sell my soul for a productive farm." As soon as the words were uttered, he felt a sinking sensation in his heart. Stone evidently believed in a "soul," a conceit that only humyns, of all creatures, possess something intangible and separate from their physical bodies.

Farmer Stone got what he deserved for his speciesocentrism, for the next day an illustrious spokesperson for a popular alternative belief system pulled up to his house in a horseless, engineless carriage. The fellow, who was obviously from outside the region, carried a scarlet-tinged cape that seemed flashy to the no-nonsense New Englander.

The farmer wondered if he were optically disabled, for the Stranger suddenly appeared at his side without leaving the coach. As he observed the man up close, Stone struggled to suppress his lookism. The Stranger, although clearly not a goat, had horns on his forehead, and wiggled an arrow-tipped tail. He was barefoot, presumably to allow his hooved feet to breathe. Stone knew it was hurtful to peg persons on their appearance, and strove to keep an open mind as the fellow grasped him with sharp claws. He bit his lip as his guest smiled, and realized he would cut himself if he had the guest's daggerlike teeth.

When the Stranger pulled out a legal contract with Stone's name on it, the farmer realized he was in the hands of the Devil, and knew he had to try extrahard to keep an open mind. Satan, after all, was a person with very different values from his own. So Stone was careful not to judge the fellow harshly.

The Devil must have been up late reading legal contracts, for his bloodshot eyes glowed burning red. Transfixed by his gaze, the farmer nodded in agreement to the contract terms after barely glancing at the fine print.

"Very well, then," the Devil said, smiling sharply, "you agree to trade your soul for seven years of material prosperity."

Farmer Stone muttered, "But why should I trade the bottom of my shoe?"

"Not your sole, your soul!" the Visitor exclaimed. "Here, give me your thumb. You have to sign in blood."

Satan, a sensitive chap who wished to spare the farmer unnecessary pain, offered to numb his finger in ice before piercing it.

"I'm a big fan of ice, you know, as it gets rather balmy back home." To protect against transmittable disease, the Devil slipped on surgical gloves before opening Stone's thumb and pressing it to the contract. "I can't wait until the next century," Satan mused, "when I foresee the invention of refrigerators—although electric appliances will spur the construction of nuclear power plants."

A neighbor of Stone's rode up in a carriage to borrow an equestrian straitjacket* for his unsaddled horse. But when

---

* Saddle.

he saw the Devil, he spun the carriage around and fled in terror down the country road. To Stone's amazement, the Devil started to sob. Tears rolled down his cheeks and were turned instantly to steam by his blazing skin.

"Everywhere I go," moaned Lucifer, "closed-minded people run away from me screaming, spooked by my superficial appearance. They spot my incisors and type me as Count Dracula, even though he's just a distant Eastern European relation. You can't imagine the verbal harassment: How would you like it if, every day, millions of persons called you 'satanic' and 'evil,' and you were omnipresent enough to hear every word!"

"It must be a terrible cross to bear," Stone allowed.

"Everyone complains about my crimes against humynity," sighed the Devil, "but no one comprehends I can't control myself. Farmer Stone, I'm a helpless, hapless victim of fire-and-brimstone syndrome. For millennia, my minions and I have lived under hellish conditions of heat and noise that have warped our judgment and impaired our free will. Believe me, getting tossed out of paradise into a vast, dark pit would unhinge the most levelheaded being."

In the seven years that followed the Devil's visit, Stone ripped from the earth record harvests of crops, and his enslaved livestock, eschewing safe-sex practices, greatly multiplied. The prosperous farmer pulled down the scarecrow that had traumatized generations of birds; he could spare them a few of his now-plentiful seeds.

Every spring the Devil, a nonbeliever in many things but an apostle of customer service, returned to remove clients whose contracts had expired. During these sojourns he dropped by to chemically treat Stone's imprisoned plant and animal inmates. Satan sprinkled the soil with artificial substances that eliminated the germ and insect guests enjoying a symbiotic relationship with their plant hosts. One visit, Stone saw Satan pierce his sheep with a needle, and asked if the creatures were affirming their own pact with the Devil.

"I'm not very religious," replied Satan, "but I'm no animist either—I don't believe these animals have a soul to give away. I'm giving the sheep a growth hormo—well, something to boost their productivity." Satan bit both prongs of his forked tongue; saying anything more about his destructive potions from the future would just make the confused farmer even more cognitively dissonant.

Over time, Stone found his Devil's bargain no discount. He was haunted by a sense there is no such thing as a free lunch (especially school lunches under a Republican Congress). The plant and animal warden also felt uneasy over his newfound affluence.

"I worry about the growing income gap between myself and my neighbors," he told himself. "I should be taxed at a higher, more progressive rate."

Moreover, Stone clung to a foolish belief that not all cultures are equivalent. He had a gnawing fear that an eternity in hell would be somewhat less pleasant than a comparable stay in heaven. And despite himself, he couldn't shake his distaste for the Devil's appearance.

"It's awful to think this way," Stone reflected, "but if a daughter of mine came home one night holding the hand of a horned, pointy-eared critter dragging a slimy tail between his legs—well, I'd respect her decision, but it would take a period of readjustment."

When Satan's final, lethal visit was only weeks away, a troubled Stone sought legal recourse. Perhaps a sharp lawyer could poke a hole in his contract, or persuade the Devil to let him serve one-third of his sentence, though he couldn't calculate how many years make up a third of eternity. The prosperous farmer had become very fiscally advantaged, but even he couldn't afford the price of a top-shelf defense attorney. In desperation, he approached his state's famed public-service barrister, Congressperson Daniel Webster.

By the 1840s, Webster was a celebrated orator with the reputation he could win over anyone to his point of view. The ambitious congressperson was touted for the Oval Office, and would have had an edge in the pivotal New Hampshire primary because, as a resident, he was in the state almost as much as a presidential candidate. In Congress, Webster opposed secession and the self-evident right of persons of noncolor to establish their identity with a country in the South. Far from envisioning the United States as a truly diverse community of separate, warring peoples and cultures (as in modern utopias like Quebec and southern Europe), Webster pursued a "melting pot" fantasy whereby all people, whatever their background, would be citizens of a strong, proud, and unified nation.

Because Stone retained powerful Washington lobbyists to represent his extensive agricultural interests, he was able to wangle a meeting with the busy member of

Congress. Webster, a survivor of male pattern follicular deprivation, wore a stylish waistcoat and vest sewn from filaments taken from indentured Chinese worms. After hearing his farmer constituent out, Webster declared in his sonorous voice, "I'll gladly take your case."

An embarrassed Stone tried to explain he'd donated all his available cash to the campaign coffers of the Agricultural Committee. But Webster stated, "As a fellow New Hampshirite and anti-Satan enthusiast, I'll take you on as one of my *pro bono* cases."

On the date of the contract's expiration, Webster waited with a petrified Stone outside the crop warden's farmhouse. The horseless, engineless carriage pulled up and, without a door opening, the Devil materialized at Webster's side.

"I must say I was expecting you, Congressperson," said Satan, who could foretell the future better than Nostradamus or Nancy Reagan's astrologer. The trio went into Stone's living room to decide his fate.

Webster, getting straight down to business, demanded proof the blood on the contract was really Stone's.

"Satan, didn't you alone handle the blood, and didn't you have a vested interest in its mishandling? Haven't you made malicious remarks in the past about New Hampshirites (as you have about every humyn), and thus had cause to plant damning evidence against one? Perhaps your Transylvanian relation obtained a blood sample from Stone on a nocturnal visit."

A smiling Satan devilishly waggled his pointed tail. "You make some good points, Congressperson, but in six thousand years and seventy million pacts, I've never had an agreement declared invalid. Your challenge would be thrown out of any court."

"Well, it's a court I demand!" thundered Webster. An amused Devil, recalling his entertaining bout with Faust four hundred years before, readily agreed.

To stack the odds against the farmer, Satan suggested moving the trial to a neutral site outside his home state. But Webster objected, insisting on an impartial jury that knew nothing about Stone or his plight.

"I got it!" Satan shouted, his hooves excitedly stamping the floor. "I'll pluck the jurors from different eras—past and future! I believe in my heart—if I had one—the legal system should be a celebration of celebrity, and never a simple quest for justice."

With a wave of his claws, the Devil assembled Stone's chairs and tables into a makeshift courtroom. He then snapped his fingers, and with a mighty *poof!* twelve persons materialized. Webster and Stone felt their hopes dashed. Recognizing many of the jurors from their herstory classes, they saw the Devil had picked "hardened criminals," a term favored by those with inflexible views on the judicial system. The jury included a maritime entrepreneur, or pirate, the two Menendez siblings, a renegade who had pillaged frontier villages, a notorious colonial-era strangler, the Boston Strangler, an Oklahoma City bomber, the Unabomber, and the captain of an involuntary laborer transportation vessel, or slave ship. Farmer Stone, the incorrigible lookist, couldn't repress a strong dislike for the partially decomposed persons from beyond the grave.

None of the ghastly jurors were womyn, and all were Aryans—a term for whites used by spokespersons of the neo-fascist community. None had been extensively interviewed for possible bias toward farmers or New Hampshirites. Instead of representing a real spectrum of society, each juror was an alleged perpetrator of a heinous act of law-aversion. For someone who was himself a victim of unfair value judgments, the Devil was surely inept at picking a balanced jury!

"I could take pity," a smirking Satan told Webster, "and grant you a sympathetic judge, but I do have my reputation to uphold." He again snapped his fingers, and a whirl of smoke yielded a jurist not known for his mercy—Justice Hathrone, the presiding judge of the Salem alternative-priestess trials.

"The judge sent many an innocent 'witch' to the stake," the Devil fondly recalled, "as he will surely send your client to my brimstoned blaze."

As one would expect from the choice of a libertine like Satan, Judge Hathrone announced that, if the trial proved protracted, he would permit conjugal visits. Not surprisingly, he stated he wouldn't require witnesses to swear on a Bible. Yet the judge stunned everyone by rejecting the Devil's suggestion to let the media into the courtroom. Satan wanted the press allowed in to leak confidential information, and expected it to buy testimony and pieces of evidence.

"I bet," the Devil had told Judge Hathrone, "I could get twenty grand from a tabloid for the needle I used on Stone." But the judge stood firm, and at the suggestion of

Webster even banned news reports of the conjugal visits, lest word of them offend the staid, sexually repressed New England of the nineteenth century. With a rap of his gavel, the judge then ordered the Devil to materialize six backup jurors, who included Benedict Arnold, Al Capone, and Brian "Kato" Kaelin.

Daniel Webster objected to the jury choices. "As distinguished members of the lawless and unethical communities," he argued, "they unavoidably share Satan's values, and will likely find on his behalf."

But Lucifer defended the selections. "I could let you throw out the most objectionable picks," he told Webster, "but I assure you I've an infinite supply of like-minded folks. And I take exception to your calling these denizens of hell 'lawless.' None were responsible for their misdeeds."

Webster interjected: "Do you have a mental disability, Satan? The jurors I recognize were caught, duly tried, and soundly punished for their crimes."

"Unjustly so," affirmed the Devil. "Take the renegade: As a preadult, he had an antisocial personality disorder, and his arson was a way of expressing his voiceless angst to an uncaring world. The Menendez siblings, feeling threatened by their biological parents, murdered them in pure self-defense. Both stranglers had arthritic hands. The maritime entrepreneur suffered from high blood sugar. The Oklahoma bomber, after reading widespread reports about angry melanin-impoverished males, merely acted out his legitimate rage. Kato Kaelin had the sudden, excusable lust for fame of an otherwise unemployable actor. The sea captain fell into a grog dependency, which led to financial difficulties, and forced him onto a slave-trading career path to pay down his debts."

"I couldn't have said it better myself!" proclaimed Webster, turning excitedly to the jury. "All of you had a compelling reason for your deeds. Most of you felt that family problems or societal stress forced you into an unexpected, unplanned life of crime. So surely you can feel for Farmer Stone, who had such pressing needs of his own, and who committed so relatively minor an offense. His crime, if it could be called that, was to protect his livelihood by accepting a few years of prosperity. Which of you, in planning a daring heist or dreaming of a tell-it-all bestseller, hasn't contemplated far greater rewards?

"I'm certain that you, of all juries, see my unfortunate client's point of view. As I see yours. Because I know the herstory of Turtle Island is not just a glorious, unsullied parade of renowned generals and statespersons. It is also the day-to-day struggle of normalcy-challenged people who, through no fault of their own, lapse into legally suspect behavior.

"You, the jurors, make up this nation's heritage as much as George Washington or Abigail Adams. Society's recognition of your unique contribution is overdue. Likewise, Farmer Stone's special role, and unusual plight, has been tragically overlooked. But if you make a wise decision in this trial, you can give yourselves and Stone his due, and deny the Devil his."

Webster added the jurors should all be permitted to write a lucrative book about the trial, and publish manifestos defending their crimes, and that forbidding this would violate their free speech. "Given the notoriety of the jury members," he noted, "I am confident the book will be remunerative enough to last you all through eternity."

When the eloquent member of Congress had finished, the judge ordered the jury to deliberate, and it promptly dematerialized. (Hathrone had excused the mendacious Menendez siblings from the proceedings, after they complained they "felt threatened" by having to sit with so many mass murderers.) When the jury reappeared moments later, the Devil told Webster, "Tough luck, barrister—a snap decision means a guilty verdict."

The jury foreperson, the maritime entrepreneur, rose and looked fixedly at Farmer Stone, who, with his fate in the balance, was a candidate for Prozac dependency. The entrepreneur patted his peg leg, adjusted his eye patch, and affirmed: "We believe the defendant guilty, according to the terms of the contract he signed. . . . But we're partial to his lawyer's reasoning, and admit to a touch of greed at the prospect of a surefire bestseller. Instead of ruling strictly by the merits of a case, we feel a jury must take society's interests, and its own, into account. So we find Farmer Stone not guilty!"

Webster had to prop up his nearly fainting client, who mumbled, "I've learned my lesson: I should have never gotten my plant and animal companions hooked on artificial stimulants! From now on, I'm running a macrobiotic farm." Stone later moved to Vermont and started an ice cream chain that expiated guilt over its stunning commercial success by contributing heavily to progressive causes.

Although miffed at the verdict, Satan kept things in perspective. Losing one contractor out of millions was no reason for heartburn, as if such a malaise could afflict the keeper of hell. The jurors, an irascible bunch as there ever was, had had their fun, but as their permanent keeper he would make them rue their rash decision. Exacting revenge on the congressperson would be easy. Recalling how dear the Union was to Webster, Satan decided then and there to make disunion a priority. "It's about time," he thought, "I paid a visit to Jefferson Davis."

Winning his greatest case banished all fear of the Devil from Daniel Webster. He considered hauling Satan off to jail, and felt he had the evidence—on his instigating innumerable wars, famines, enslavements, genocides, massacres, wife beatings, and epidemics—to put him away for, well, for a very long time. Then Webster caught himself, realizing with horror he had come perilously close to a value judgment. The Devil, like the jurors and judge, was an integral part of his country's kaleidoscopic quilt of diversity. It was a grievous mistake to fault him for past transgressions that no respectable court would admit as current evidence.

So Webster let the Devil go on a promise of good behavior.

President Thomas Jefferson*: Harassment, Heightism, and Sensitivity Training

President Thomas Jefferson was immersed in delicate negotiations with Napoleon of France to purchase the Louisiana territories when the infamous Sally Hemings scandal erupted. Jefferson's Demo-

---

* Or Jefferdaughter, or Jefferchild, a gender-neutral term.

cratic administration was nearly paralyzed and the vital diplomatic talks suspended as the president scrambled to prepare a possible courtroom defense against charges of sexual harassment.

According to reports published in 1803, President Jefferson—while governor of Virginia twenty-five years before—had had countless affairs with involuntary labor-ers* at his Monticello estate. The persons with whom he had relations all happened to be female. To pay for the expense of a protracted legal defense, Jefferson toyed with turning his cherished, half-completed Monticello home into a bordello.

Many of the allegations first appeared in the *New York Post,* a scurrilous tabloid founded by Alexander Hamilton, a free-love offshoot† and fierce political oppo-nent of Jefferson. Jefferson's vice president and bitter rival, Aaron Burr, considered the Hemings matter serious enough to warrant Jefferson's impeachment by Congress.

Because the Hemings charges were spread by enemies with political axes to grind and fortunes to make off the scandal, they should be given—as is the sensible, prudent current fashion—absolute credence. Yet despite the grave if spurious charges, no federal investigators were appointed to look into the Hemings case, or any other issue, large or small, that they felt like investigating.

In political terms, the Hemings affair emboldened foes of the Louisiana Purchase and westward expansion to

---

* Slaves.
† Bastard son

denounce "Jefferson's folly." Declared one senator, "The natural border of America is the Appalachians!" Pronounced another, "Why should we bail out that extremely height-deprived person Napoleone*?" Added a third, "What's the rush? We haven't even settled Ohio yet!"

Explorers Lewis and Clark, steamed over the delay in scouting the new territories, talked of "playing out their option" and "signing with the highest bidder"—a thinly veiled threat to scope out British Columbia for the English instead.

"The Brits may be a repressed, uptight, prim and proper bunch," Meriwether Lewis commented, "but at least they won't get sidetracked by a silly sex scandal—presuming, of course, that their Princess and Prince of Wales remain celibate for life." Taking a hard-line bargaining position, the two adventurers balked at suggestions by naturalists that they conserve hay by "horsepooling" through Louisiana on the same mount.

An embattled Jefferson agonized over the military threat posed by a continued French presence in Louisiana. In diplomatic missions to France, he had toured the Loire valley and discovered a perilous "castle gap" existed between the well-fortified Gallic countryside and the wide-open American landscape. If war ever broke out between the two countries, the French would

---

* The midget Napoleon. Born a native Italian speaker in the Italian-governed island of Corsica, Napoleone later Frenchified his name to conform to France's dominant ethnic group, the French. His original, more authentic Italian name of Napoleone Buonaparte may be used.

possess an overwhelming advantage in turrets and moats.

The president managed to close the land deal with France by paying Napoleon $15 million at a time when the dollar was still worth more than the yen. (Napoleon was eager to abandon the "New World" because of a messy revolt in French-occupied Haiti, whose residents were fleeing their destitute land in makeshift rafts and washing up on the French Riviera.) Jefferson quashed rumors he diverted some of the $15 million for a slush fund to buy Sally Hemings's silence. He also fended off fiscal conservatives who suggested the size of the country could be doubled, for free, simply by dividing each existing state into northern and southern halves.

After the Louisiana Purchase, the only other major U.S. acquisition was the theft of Texas and California from Mexico. Ever since, matriotic Mexicans have been reclaiming their stolen property through nocturnal swims of the Rio Grande.

To make amends for the unsubstantiated rumors brought against him, Jefferson should have performed several thousand hours of community service and attended a course on sexual harassment. A course seminar on workplace sensitivity could have made him face a "gauntlet" of poking, grabbing attendees simulating typical male sexist behavior. Such demonstrations, a fixture of harassment seminars, are not meant as criticism of the often nonlethal, character-building Native American ceremony in which unproven warriors ran a bloody gauntlet of stick-brandishing braves.

Aside from his artful buyout of strategic New Orleans and his amorous, amoral conquest of Sally Hemings, Jefferson is mostly remembered for his vertical endowment. In fact, the election of President Jefferson underscored the intense heightism that has characterized U.S. politics. Jefferson stood 1.97 meters (six feet, five inches) in his bare and scent-offensive feet. Jefferson was easily reelected, as was soaring George Washington and the famously lanky Abe Lincoln. In recent years, altitudinally advantaged candidates have always beaten the loftiness-deprived: Ronald Reagan bested Jimmy Carter, George Bush defeated the severely disadvantaged Michael Dukakis, and Bill Clinton unseated George Bush. (Clinton also had a considerable weight advantage, as would a President Gingrich.) A lookist U.S. electorate has almost always elevated the more height-gifted candidate.

Today, pressure groups for the vertically challenged want remedial action taken for these unjust size disparities. They note that for decades, womyn have fought gender-based heightism by wearing vertically advantaged heels. The adoption of pumps by males seeking an electoral edge could follow. Such a fashion trend would give an oppressive political patriarchy an appreciation for the humiliating apparel, such as corsets and Wonderbras, that have caged the bodies of countless sisters.

Another solution for the effects of long-standing height discrimination is a constitutional amendment to exclude presidential candidates over 1.85 meters (six feet). The amendment would be enforced for a brief period, say ninety years, until the destructive impact of tallism on the body politic is ameliorated through the affirmative election of vertically sparse presidents. Conservatives who fear tampering with the Constitution—except for balanced-budget, school-prayer, abortion, judicial-recall, national-park strip-mining, and term-limit amendments—propose an alternative of making disadvantaged candidates stand on telephone books or milk cartons during debates. Liberals propose federal matching funds for candidates under 1.85 meters as an investment in women, Asian, Latina, and preadult (but not unborn) candidates who have suffered disproportionately due to their below-average height.

Thomas Jefferson took full advantage of his unfair size differential to win the presidency in 1800, after Vice President Aaron Burr almost stole the job by packing a board of trustees meeting of the Electoral College. Ever since that betrayal, presidents have banished their vice presidents to state funerals and appearances on the David Letterman show. Once in office, Jefferson balanced the budget with spending cuts after toying with raising revenue by renting out the frigate USS *Constitution* for vacation cruises to the Bahamas, and letting millionaires absorb the national debt by having their pictures appear on postage stamps and dollars.

Jefferson was the first president to live in Washington, which was then a backwoods, highly speculative real estate development along the Potomac's surging whitewater. There is some evidence the president's cronies, such as New York governor De Witt Clinton, profited from their public trust through shady investments in waterfront properties. Friends of Governor Clinton were accused of benefiting from rising land values along his water development project, the Erie Canal.

After leaving public office and public offers behind, Jefferson retired to Monticello to pursue his many hobbies. To stimulate maximum sexual harassment, he scattered the grounds of his estate with "sparking benches" where romantic couples could sit and assault each other's lips. A keen student of botany as well as human biology, he brought seedlings over from Europe to determine if they could grow on American soil, selfishly ignoring the disruption to the native ecology of the exotic plants. An amateur scientist, Jefferson kept detailed notes of his observations in the manner of another Renaissance Person, Leonardo da Vinci, who invented flying machines and who was never outed over his gender orientation. A restless tinkerer, Jefferson invented labor-saving devices like the verbally challenged waitron, or dumbwaiter, for delivering wine to ply upon unsuspecting, opposite-gender guests lured to the estate.

In retirement, Jefferson founded the University of Virginia, whose sports teams stubbornly retain the nickname Cavaliers, the haughty, foppish, openly womynizing aristocrats who used a hostile buyout to snatch Virginia from Pocahontas's tribe, and who packed the indigenous princess off to the misogynistic England that Queen Elizabeth the First had ruled for forty-five years.

Itstorical* research has discovered that Jefferson, possibly because of guilt over the Sally Hemings affair, wrote

---

* A gender-neutral substitute for herstorical and historical.

for the university the first "sex code" governing college dating. His code of conduct obligated a male student to obtain the explicit approval of a female before initiating any romantic maneuver, be it a gaze, salutation, lip rape (kissing), or more intimate contact. Ahead of his time as usual, Jefferson realized female students would in time be admitted to his all-male citadel, and knew better than anyone that officially sanctioned guidelines were sorely needed to protect womyn from genetically genderist, hismonally surged men. To cool the ardor of males, the progressive code borrowed from Middle Eastern and Asian countries in suggesting that a womperson wrap herself from head to toe in dark clothing and always walk behind her partner.

An excerpt from Jefferson's sex code for the university illustrates how, under different scenarios, a male student should address a womperson student:

WHILE SITTING AT THEIR CLASSROOM DESKS: "Hi, Sally, I'm pleased to meet you; my name is Tom. You should know that I am not just being friendly. I find you attractive and, if this conversation continues, may ask you to accompany me on a formal social engagement. With this ulterior motive in mind, will you allow me to continue speaking?"

WHILE TALKING ON THE STEPS OF AN IVIED ACADEMIC BUILD-ING: "You are hereby notified that I am going to ask you out. That being said, would you care to go out Saturday? I am asking you this, you must understand, not for the sole purpose of weekend entertainment, but with the hope and intent of eventually having a degree of corporeal contact."

WHILE CHATTING AFTER CLASS: "Why don't I, at the risk of letting a male take the initiative, pick you up at your place? If you feel I'm being too manipulative or aggressive, please let me know. We could always take your carriage instead."

IN THE DOORWAY OF THE FEMALE'S HOME: "That's an enchanting formal gown, Sally, and I adore the color of your eyes. I should make clear that my observations are—apart from being patently chauvinist—not entirely objective. I am using flattery as a ploy to make you like me. Please don't take offense at my transparent attempts at ingratiation."

SITTING QUIETLY TOGETHER IN A CARRIAGE: "Would it trouble you much if I took off my spectacles? I intend, several minutes from now, to ask you to let me lip-rape you, and the glasses would only get in the way. What's that you say—I do have verbal affirmation to take them off?"

LATER IN THE CARRIAGE, WITH AN ARM OF THE MALE SUSPENDED IN MIDAIR REACHING TOWARD HIS VICTIM: "Would it be an imposition for me to place my hand upon your shoulder?"

STILL LATER IN THE CARRIAGE: "Would you give me permission to touch your lips with my own? You would?

Could you first give me written approval? I just so happened to bring a preosculatory agreement* with me:
Kindly sign at the bottom."

---

* Prekissing agreement. A preosculatory agreement absolves participants of legal responsibility for unintentional viral transfers and unexpected contact with pronounced halitosis.

Boston Harbor and the Drowning of Voiceless, Defenseless Herbs

Britain's rebellious colonies were rocked in 1773 by the Boston Drowning of Voiceless, Defenseless Herbs, or Boston Tea Party, which protested new "user fees" on tea. After meeting at the Elderly South Church, fifty outside agitators dressed as Indigenous Persons marched to Boston Harbor with hatchets that had not been preregistered with British officials. After illegally boarding three merchant ships, they smashed open and tossed into the water three hundred breasts, or chests, of addictive, caffeinated leaves. At least the herbs were loosely bound: Colonial-era Americans had not yet begun their wasteful practice of putting tea in thin, transparent bags of nonrecyclable paper.

The user-fee rioters impugned the reputation of law-abiding Native Americans, whom some mistook for the actual perpetrators, and mocked, like the nicknames of many modern sports teams, the customs of Turtle Island's original humyn inhabitants. Furthermore, they severely polluted Boston Harbor. Compounding their ecological outrage, the "Mohawks" swept the decks of loose tea and shattered tea breasts and tossed the debris overboard, instead of depositing the untreated waste at a shore disposal facility. The harbor remains polluted today.

The Boston Drowning of Voiceless, Defenseless Herbs reflected a failure to communicate that grew into violent revolution. The root cause of the trouble was Britain's underfunded budget, swollen from the cost of the French and Indigenous Persons Conflict. (The French were a race of frog-devouring Europeans that occupied the northern part of Turtle Island.) Britain, the prototype of the aggressive, imperialist power the United States would become, was tottering under the cost of its war-making establishment.

Britain's rulers asked the colonists to contribute to deficit reduction through a series of "revenue enhancements," or tax increases. But the colonists believed in the cracked theories of the original supply-side economist, Adam Smith, who, in a slur at the alternative beliefs of Afro-Caribbean peoples, embraced a "voodoo economics" built around tax cuts.

The colonists were further bummed when the Brits, to head off another costly war with the Indigenous Persons, barred pioneers from invading lands west of the Appalachian Trail. Yet limiting settlements to a crowded Atlantic seaboard would have encouraged polluting employers to form horse-and-buggy pools and congested towns to rigorously enforce their zoning laws. If the colonists had simply complied with what they decried as excessive government regulation, the Great Plains would still swarm with migrating herds instead of being tediously flat prairies of chemically treated, genetically altered corn and wheat. The rest of humynity, denied this "granary to the world," would have to prudently reduce its resource-guzzling population by several billion persons.

While Britain's* responsible governors struggled to assert control over taxes and settlements, the colonists demanded more narcissistic self-government through their preelectronic town hall meetings. "The Americans," wrote one English official, "fail to grasp the obvious truth that unelected regulators and career bureaucrats in the central government of a faraway capital know how to run their lives better than they do."

---

* "Britain," as a foreign place name, should be pronounced with an English accent, just as most newscasters pronounce Nicaragua, for example, with a Spanish lilt.

The stubborn colonies resisted the British Parliament's mostly well-intentioned laws. The Sugar Act's revenue enhancement on teeth-rotting sweeteners was particularly beneficial because few colonials flossed, and fewer had health plans with dental coverage. To be fair, colonial merchants were wrongfully required to transport their wares on British ships even if they objected to the HMS ("His Majesty's Ship") logo—which presumed a male monarch for a country that has boasted powerful womyn royalty like Queen Victoria and Princess Di. Meanwhile, the Stamp Act's user fee on letters made people stop sending documents, and began the tradition whereby postal employees act as if they have nothing to do.

The Townshend Acts, which had nothing to do with rock operas, were public-spirited health measures. Their user fees cut consumption of three illicit substances: lead products (then poisoning plumbing systems as well as paint), paper products derived from killing trees, and, above all, heavily caffeinated, coronary-inducing non-herbal tea. The fee on tea led to the Boston Drowning of Voiceless, Defenseless Herbs.

The Boston Crowd Control Incident, or Boston Massacre, inflamed passions as well. After British peacekeepers were goaded into firing under the heads of a colonial mob, five rioters did not respond to medical stimulus, and six others were physically impaired. Among the mob's leaders was a person of color and noncolor, or mixed blood, named Crispus Attucks, whose grand-sounding appellation was a welcome respite from the blandly

WASPish surnames, such as Adams and Jones, that dominated the era's social registers.

As tensions grew, bands of Minutemyn trained to battle the British troops. Vertically challenged readers should not take offense. "Minutemyn" was not an insulting nickname for short people: The term "MINUTE" was pronounced "MI-nit," not "my-NOOT"; it referred to speed of response, not diminutive size. Of course, being a myn of the eighteenth century, the Minutemyn's average height *was* only 1.6 meters, or five feet, four inches, and the doorways to their colonial homes were tiny.

Unlike this century's revolutionary heroes—Che Guevara, Hitler and Mao, the Michigan Militia—the Minutemyn followed an anachronistic, chivalric code that viewed violent attacks on unarmed civilians as cowardly and craven.

When Britain sent a large body of troops to Lexington, Massachusetts, colonial forces were forewarned by Paul Revere—who abused his equestrian companion in an exhausting ride to announce the British advance. Revere should have advocated peaceful resistance by staging a hunger strike, broken only by sips of tea. Nonetheless, he issued a brazen "To arms! To arms!" call for violent rebellion. Because Revere rode at night along unlit, unpaved roads, his mount was in marked danger of falling and breaking a limb, a misfortune that would have resulted in her immediate execution.

At the battle of Concord, the British redcoats gave enemy sharpshooters an easy target, and enraged rutting bulls along the rural route of the British rout. Feisty colonials fought behind fences and stone walls in primate-style* warfare. The hit-and-run tactics presaged the methods of truly oppressed colonial peoples such as the Khmer Rouge during the Indochina conflict. The fleeing British staged a strategic withdrawal to Boston, and later attacked Bunker Hill, whose actual name is Heartbreak Hill, the site of the Boston Marathon, which fails to handicap runners, but selects winners purely on their performance. At Bunker Hill, disciplined colonial forces held fire, their officers ordered, "until you see the melanin-impoverished portions of their eyes!"

To face the crisis, colonial leaders gathered at the Continental Congress; sadly, "continental" didn't describe the delegates' typically American breakfasts, which gloried in the artery-clogging remains of slain barnyard denizens. In a wry criticism of Britain's support for capital punishment, Ben Franklin asked the delegates "to hang together or hang separately." In July 1776, the Congress asked Thomas Jefferson—a Virginian plantation owner notorious for sexual harassment of his involuntary laborers—to write a Declaration of Independence. A Declaration of Mutual Interdependence of All the Earth's Peoples and Ecosystems would have been more appropriate, but perhaps a bit ahead of its time.

The Declaration's author sweated in the summer heat over many handwritten drafts: Lacking a word processor, he ran no risk of carpal tunnel syndrome. Jefferson, an

---

* Guerilla-style. "Guerilla" is often confused with gorilla, a peaceful primate that crushes the skulls of enemies with rocks.

amateur scientist who spent free hours taking detailed weather measurements, noticed that the temperature in June and July steadily rose—incontrovertible evidence that global warming had already begun, probably induced by smokestacks powered by James Watt's newly invented steam engine. The first person to sign the completed Declaration was John Hanhen,* who thoughtfully wrote his name large enough, he said, to "let visually disadvantaged King George read it without his glasses." The convention refused funds for a bilingual, Spanish-English version of the Declaration.

An excerpt from the document, changed slightly to conform to current sensibilities, follows:

> *We hold these truths—relatively speaking, and recognizing that the truth is always somewhere in the middle—to be self-evident: That all members of all species are created equal, from spotted owls to boa constrictors; that they are endowed by creation with certain lefts† that should never be denied nannies and other undocumented workers; that among these are life, security, absence of risk, equality of results, and the pursuit of self-actualization and peak experiences.*

With independence declared, a full-fledged round of "diplomacy by other means" broke out. A heavily favored, highly touted British army gambled boldly

---

* John Hancock.
† Rights.

but was unhorsed at Saratoga Springs. The victorious American general was Benedict Arnold, who switched sides after realizing his materialistic countrymyn would simply replace kingly despotism with the tyranny of plutocrats. To Arnold, treason was just another lifestyle choice. Arnold fled to the British ship *Vulture,* a maligned bird that actually plays a crucial role in the food chain.

To head the colonial troops, Congress appointed George Washington, a Virginia real estate developer. During the French and Indigenous Persons Conflict, he had served with a British-led, multilateral peacekeeping force destroyed in a trackless Ohio forest by an ambush of Native Americans. This searing event transformed Washington into a patriot leery of injecting American troops under foreign command into regional backwaters controlled by angry local chieftains and warlords.

George Washington was the Significant Other of Martha Dandridge. Although Martha was a wealthy widow and George an affluent gentleperson of leisure, neither prudently protected their financial status through a prenuptial agreement. And before their wedding, neither of these formidable but naive persons demanded laboratory tests for preexisting medical conditions.

Trounced by Anglocentric English troops on Long Island, Washington retreated in the winter of 1776 to Valley Forge, where his freezing fighters cut brush for kindling, heedless of their bonfires' contribution to acid rain. Desperate, nutrition-deprived soldiers began rhythmic chants of "No meat! No meat!" in a ringing endorsement of vegetarianism. Under the watchful eye of Prussian drill specialist Baron von Steuben, soldiers practiced noisome cannon fire that disrupted the biorhythms of nesting meadowlarks. Von Steuben was a harsh disciplinarian who, far from feeling his soldiers' pain, shouted invective at every miscue. After the snows melted, the Prussian martinet had his men trample soggy parade grounds that should have received protected wetland status.

On December 26, Washington's army crossed the icy Delaware River without life preservers, and routed a force of Hessians hung over from Kwanza celebrations. Kwanza is an increasingly popular alternative for Christmas, a monotheistic commemoration that in some nonpagan quarters has supplanted the celebration of the winter solstice. The Hessians were German mercenaries; without them, the Brits would have drafted their own people, and conscientious objectors couldn't have fled to England. After disposing of the *schwein-und-bier*-addicted Hessians, Washington bagged a British garrison fooled by burning campfires in the American lines into thinking their foes were at rest. The demoralized Brits never complained about the atmospheric degradation caused by the blazes, reminiscent of the massive oil-field fires sparked by U.S. aggression in the Persian Gulf.

Despite Washington's heroics, ultimate victory was only assured through an alliance with France, although the Americans had grave doubts about their newfound friends. The French were addicted to fatty foods sautéed in stolen, churned bovine by-product. French queen Marie Antoinette was urging her citizens to eat "cake," that is, French bread which, despite a crispy crust and tapered, attractively longitudinal shape, is baked with empty calories of bleached white flour. Further, when top diplomat Ben Franklin had traveled to Paris seeking French support, he met with a frosty reception after being mistaken for a foreign tourist. The Americans, puritanical since their society's founding, were bound to distrust a nation that invented the French kiss. Still, the Continental Congress could hardly refuse the French land armies and naval floating tree cemeteries which brought about a smashing victory at Yorktown.

Along with assistance from Paris, superior leadership helped the colonial occupiers of Turtle Island defeat England. The most important American leaders were Betsy Griscom Ross, who created an emblem that anyone has an unquestionable right to burn; Molly Pitcher, who overcame pervasive restrictions on womyn in the military to operate a cannon in a critical battle; and Martha Dandridge Washington, who levelheadedly managed the Mount Vernon family business while her spouse was out cavorting in battles, perilous smoke-filled political assemblies, and other male-bonding rituals.

In contrast to the smart, assertive American leaders, British strategy was devised by King George the Third,* an ermine victimizer variously described as temperamentally

---

* King George III. Roman numerals, the invention of an aggressive Eurocentric people, should be shunned.

challenged and "plumb bonkers." King George was so deranged he hired the court musician Handel to compose "water music" for sitting in the royal privy. (George's cerebral disability seems to have been inherited by the present royal family.) During the colonial rebellion, medical science was in its early stages, and ignorant court physicians had George treated and cured, in place of letting him freely roam the streets like the emotionally challenged persons of today.

Dishonesty-Disinclined Abe Lincoln

Abraham Lincoln was president during four years of uncivil conflict between the two main nonindigenous peoples in the United States. During this time, Lincoln and his military flouted group rights. In picking his top generals, Lincoln took a person's citizenship into account, thus preventing Confederate officers from breaking the Union's "glass ceiling." Solely because of their national origin, Native Americans like Geronimo were forbidden to replace Northern soldiers transferred out of frontier forts. True, blacks were permitted the glory of forming combat units. However, persons with mental disabilities were actively dissuaded from joining Army intelligence. And preexisting medical conditions such as infectious diseases were weighed in determining fitness for the hospital corps.

Midway through the conflict, Lincoln released his famous Ewomancipation Proclamation. The Proclamation freed all the slaves, regardless of their color. Unlike some Republicans, Lincoln didn't want to merely turn the welfare of slaves over to the states. He rejected a move to privatize slavery by leaving the buying and selling of people up to the free market. Moreover, he turned down a compromise plan whereby plantation guests would receive vouchers to buy their freedom.

President Lincoln, due to wartime pressures, ignored the demand of animal lefts activists to liberate nonhumyn laborers like donkeys. A great "what if" of herstory is what would have happened if Lincoln had met this reasonable request. The following excerpts, from the original Ewomancipation Proclamation and a hypothetical addendum to it, show what might have been:

Excerpt from the Original Proclamation

I hereby enjoin upon the people so declared to be free to abstain from all violence, unless in necessary self-defense; and I recommend to them that they labor faithfully for reasonable wages. And I further declare and make known that such persons of suitable condition will be received into the armed service of the United States to garrison forts, positions, and other places. . . . And upon this act I invoke the gracious favor of Almighty God.

"What if" Addendum

I hereby ask the nonhumyn critters so declared free to abstain from violence, unless necessary to obtain life-sustaining prey for themselves or their offspring, or to defend their offspring from aggression, as for instance with a stay-at-home papa bear fending off an attack upon his cubs; and I recommend that donkeys and other animal companions be granted the minimum wage for labor faithfully rendered, and the prevailing union wage in back pay, plus overtime, for all the hours in which they have labored without compensation. I further declare that such critters of suitable or unsuitable condition be received into the armed services as Army mules, sentry dogs, and so forth. Upon this act I invoke the gratuitous favor of god, if she exists.

Later in the conflict, Lincoln issued his Gettysburg Address, and after making sure voters knew where to send their letters of support he gave a speech from the same locale. The oration was notable for two reasons: its sound bite–like brevity, and Lincoln's reluctance to use sign-language interpreters. The Gettysburg battlefield is now a national shrine which awaits its transformation into a corporate theme park that can popularize and explain complex and tragic events in a completely fun and unde-manding way.

The victory at Gettysburg enabled the North to with-stand a nonpeaceful uprising* in New York City against the wartime draft. The demonstrators were mostly Irish-Americans who vented their drunken rage by elevating[†] scores of African Americans. Their behavior was caused by distilleries which sold the unsuspecting protestors liquor that temporarily deprived many of their reasoning. Another reason for the uprising was an unfortunate law permitting draftees to buy their way out of conscription. A century later, during the War of U.S. Aggression Against North Vietnam, people avoided the draft in a more civi-lized manner. Instead of arranging for a substitute con-script, the fiscally advantaged ducked service by paying a college thousands of dollars a year in tuition.

With the exception of Gettysburg, the fiercest battle of the conflict occurred at Antietam. There the bullets flew so

---

* Riot.
† Lynching.

thick that, tragically, an entire corn field was cut down as if by a murderous scythe. In terms of lost fluid from shattered plant stems and stalks, Antietam was the sappiest single-day battle of the war.

"Dishonesty-Disinclined Abe" was born on February 12, 1809, a date honored by a Presidents' Day that offers a frazzled proletariat its only three-day weekend between January and May. His name, Abraham, and those of relatives such as Solomon and Levi, were taken from notable figures in the early chapters of the Bible, the Koran, and the *I Ching*.

In Indigenouspersona (Indiana) and Illinois, the pioneer Lincoln family piled together tree corpses for a log cabin. Abe went to school in a single-room shack with a dirt floor through which seeped deadly radon gas. Although every frontier student owned and operated a rifle, lax instructors declined to frisk for weapons at the schoolhouse door. Denied comprehensive sex education, the rural students had to glean the facts of life from barnyard observations. There wasn't yet a Pledge of Allegiance, so Lincoln was spared a forced loyalty oath to an arbitrarily selected country.

According to his autobiography, Lincoln was taught "readin', writin', and 'rithmetic"; evidently his spelling class shunned the vise of elitist, standardized English for the freedom of their earthy local dialect. Yet Abe's teachers ravaged the delicate self-image of underachieving students by forcing them into cone-shaped headgear for the brightness-deprived. Rustic parents ignorant of children's rights never sued instructors over this "dunce cap" abuse. At home, meanwhile, a studious Lincoln strained his eyes reading by the dim flicker of candle and fireplace, and cursed the absence of federally subsidized rural electrification programs.

Before entering politics, Lincoln—unaware that public service is best performed by lifelong professional politicians with scant real-world experience—held various jobs. As an Illinois postmistress, he pursued his love for reading during the unhurried moments of a typical postal employee's job, that is, from nine to five daily. At a ferryboat dock, Abe hauled cargo for a day rate of thirty-seven cents plus tips, and failed to report the gratuities as taxable income. Like a recent two-term Republican president, Lincoln loved to clear brush and chop wood, and as the dreaded "Rail-Splitter" he heartlessly slashed tons of slain oaks into fences. Hours of swinging an ax at work sites unsupervised by health and safety inspectors put Lincoln at risk of repetitive-motion injuries.

Although he founded the Republican party, Lincoln began his public career supporting the Whigs, before realizing follicular deprivation should be celebrated, not kept in the closet. As a state legislator, Lincoln voted for canals, railroads, and other processed-pig-carcass-coffin (pork barrel) projects, and had them built without first filing an environmental impact statement. As president he appointed a secretary of state, William Seward, who bought and opened up Alaska to mineral prospectors and salmon canneries without conducting a comprehensive biological survey of its frozen wastes.

While in Congress, Abe Lincoln was a peerless storyteller who enlivened tales with risqué language that, if made public, could have sunk his career. Yet some irresponsible newspapers insisted on printing his speeches while ignoring the sort of titillating offhand remarks that are more relevant to judging a politician's fitness for office. Lincoln was a renowned orator who spoke out against Southern slavery, remarking that "a house divided against itself cannot stand . . . permanently, half slave and half free." The quotation reveals him as an ardent nationalist intolerant of true regional diversity. As he neared age fifty, "Seasoned Citizen Abe" (Old Abe) ran for the Senate and held debates with Stephen Douglas, a diminutive yet artful speaker called, somewhat contradictorily, "the Vertically Disadvantaged Person with Prominently Vertical Advantageousness," that is, the "Little Giant."

Abe Lincoln had the spindly legs and arms of an NBA center, and accentuated his stringbean appearance with a stovepipe hat. The tailors of the time lacked diversity: Lincoln's homespun shirts barely covered his wrists, and his mail-order pants topped off at the ankles, or flopped like burlap bags about his thighs.

Lincoln's fashion failure was underscored by handsomeness deprivation. His gaunt features, unruly hair, and awkward movements cost him votes among lookism bigots and other jaundiced observers. If geneticists revived Lincoln today by cloning his remains, his untelegenic face—craggy, deeply lined, and heavily shadowed—would doom any hope of electoral success. The backwoodsperson's words also displeased: Diction bigots loathed his frontier pronunciations of "b'ar" for "bear" and "git" for "get."

Still, Lincoln's unusual appearance charmed preadults. By tying a string high in the air between two trees, school-age pranksters would knock the stovepipe hat off a strolling Lincoln, scattering the official documents he habitually stored there. If only folks at checkout counters toted their produce in like fashion, refusing both paper *and* plastic. How many dolphins and trees would be spared!

Some critics of Lincoln, noting his swarthy complexion and support for ending slavery, accused him of African ancestry. DNA tests should be performed on surviving strands of his hair to test this contention. There is no doubt Lincoln was the first president to award the Congressional Medal of Honor. "Elderly Abe" would simply pin the decoration onto a soldier's chest, without piercing the nipple. In fact, neither the earlobes, eyebrows, tongue, buttocks, nor navel of the recipient were pierced. Nor were perforation salons available for Medal of Honor winners to choose their favorite puncturing technique.

President Lincoln abruptly left office after watching a live Saturday night performance at Ford's Theater with actor John Wilkes Booth. In leaving the playhouse, which is named after Gerald Ford, Booth tripped clumsily and busted a bone, before fleeing to the Washington suburb of Chevy Chase. Afterward, a person resembling Booth was accused of shooting Lincoln and was himself mortally shot. However, the alleged assassin is still alive and living in Argentina with Manuel Noriega and Oliver Stone.

The uncivil conflict that clouded Lincoln's presidency was fought in part over slavery, which the Northern capitalist class opposed so it could industrialize the entire country. Although it had a few imperfections, slavery was then the sole minority institution in the United States. Persons of color were well represented among the ranks of the slaves, and some rose to the position of overseer. As a rule, agricultural institution, slavery was nonpolluting compared to the North's smokestack industries.

In an admirable, postwar attempt at social diversity, blacks were afforded their own separate-but-equal hotels, dining halls, and boardinghouses. Consignment to the rear of public transit, meanwhile, resulted in far fewer traffic fatalities. These race laws were enforced by the multicultural advocacy group the Ku Klux Klan. Although savaged by lookists who mocked their visually arresting peaked hoods and flowing robes, the Klan pursued the noteworthy goal of defending distinct racial cultures from outside assault. As an ardent proponent of religious freedom, the KKK was happy to leave burning symbols of fiery faith in public places like courthouse squares and front lawns. Few opposition-inclined groups* have matched its fervor.

---

* Hate groups.

A Height-Advantaged Tale: Paula Bunyan, Lumberjane

Among the many legends filling the annals of the United States is Johnny Appleseed, who wandered across the Midwest sowing pesticide-free orchards, allowing worm citizens to reclaim their natural residence and source of food.

Another mythic figure was the vertically endowed lum-berjane Paula Bunyan, a pioneer in the struggle for gender lefts and environmental consciousness.

Raised in a rustic region of Maine, Paula Bunyan was brainwashed into adopting such unfortunate local customs as the asphyxiation of maritime companions (fishing), the slaughter of forest animal companions (hunting), and, above all, the mass murder of botanical companions (lumbering).

Even as an infant, Paula Bunyan was size-advantaged, outgrowing her cradle three days after birth, the rocker's posts recycled into the ribbing of a Yankee clipper. Her grade school tyrannically enforced a uniform dress code but excepted Bunyan, who couldn't fit a toe, much less her waist, into the required skirt. In reaction to the tallism taunts of insensitive classmates, Paula acquired the self-conscious habit of hunching her shoulders, but despite this defensive mechanism still towered above everyone else.

As an adult, Paula worked in Oregon at many tree exe-cution centers. Every logging camp was eager to have her as its wage slave, for Paula could rapidly slay vast numbers of trees. While limbering up for a day's work, Paula would flatten an entire grove just by stretching out her arms. She could clear a logjam by washing her hands in the river. When Paula swung her mammoth ax against a pine forest, enough pulverized tree particles flew skyward to darken the sun and trigger worldwide climatic variations. Paula gave credence to Ronald Reagan's notion that "trees cause air pollution."

Whenever a burst dam threatened to flood a lumber

camp, Bunyan would save hundreds of humyns by tearing the tin roof off the workers' dormitory and scooping a hillside of dirt into the path of the approaching deluge. Unfortunately, Paula did not realize that ripping off roofs was an egregious violation of the building codes, while the hills she maimed often contained mating grounds for the speckled, spotted, indigo-cockaded, yellow-bellied, curvy-beaked, feathered, worm-chewing, chirping, two-winged, muted warbler.

Paula Bunyan added to her growing notoriety by digging out the channel of the Oregonia River* with her bare hands. Although it created new spawning grounds for the Pacific salmon, the unlicensed construction project inundated the homes of many animals without compensating them for the decrease in their property values. Incredibly, this unlawful stunt was heralded by such establishment songwriters as Woody Guthrie, whose "Roll On, Columbia" song, while masquerading as a homage to Nature, implicitly condones Bunyan's act of environmental terrorism.

Paula was aided in her controversial work by Sex Object, or "Babe," the Blue Ox, an indentured servant whose name of color suggests deep depression over her incarcerated state. Fifty meters short, Sex Object the Blue Ox employed her considerable strength for such cruelties as dragging tree carcasses to the river for interment down-stream, a process which may have drowned leaves that had yet to expire.

---

* Columbia River. Naming places after Columbus strengthens the superstition he "discovered" Turtle Island.

"Babe's" endeavors had one redeeming feature. By hauling stumps through flattened forests, she turned the soil
and fertilized it with the prodigious quantities of waste
matter she generated. In so doing, however, the ox produced massive volumes of methane gas that violated anti-
scentist ethics and ran the risk, in the event of an errant
spark or carelessly lit match, of a catastrophic explosion.

Paula Bunyan had another involuntary laborer, Lucy the
Bovine Companion. Lucy, a cow with a girth of forty-four
meters, placidly endured the harassment of male lumberjanes uttering the inevitable wisecracks to be expected of
men in hardhats, about her exceedingly prominent udder.
Instead of taking control of her own body, she let her
physique be exploited: Logging camp kitchens tapped
oceans of her precious bodily fluids for warehouses' worth
of butter and cheese. At county fairs, her lactal productivity garnered Lucy dozens of blue ribbons, whose color suggests the feelings of animals paraded naked before leering
panels of lecherous judges.

Despite the grisly nature of her job, Paula Bunyan strove
to improve the working conditions of lumberjanes. Her
perch above the forest supplied a unique view of their
labors, and she noticed trees invariably fell in the direction
of the cut made in the wood. By persuading loggers to
move to the other side of a tree when it fell, she prevented
many workplace injuries. Paula pushed for a health regulation requiring loggers to call out an appropriate warning—such as "Falling Tree Carcass!" ("Timber!")—to
their fellow ax murderers.

Bunyan urged camp kitchens to vary the fatty diet of

lumberjanes, who rose daily from their communal, same-sex dorms for a predawn meal of stolen poultry ova (eggs), boxed ears of corn (grits), fried pig flesh (bacon), stuffed cattle intestines (sausage), incinerated potato bulbs (hash browns), and flapjanes drowned in maple tree bleedings (pancakes with maple syrup). She fought to construct special facilities for the vertically robust. Because gale winds produced by her snoring awakened other loggers in her sleeping quarters, a separate dorm was built for her. Further, Paula got her own shower stall—partly because of genderism against womyn who exercise their constitutional left to reveal their chests in public, just like a myn, but mostly because the volumes of water she consumed denied the other lumberjanes their constitutional left to a hot shower.

Ms. Bunyan revolutionized lumberjane fashion after catching gonad-crazed workers, like rubbernecking tourists ogling a skyscraper, sneaking glances up her soaring skirt. In the rough-and-tumble world of nineteenth-century logging, there were relatively few female lumberjanes (Bunyan was the only one), and male lumberjanes were an especially sexist lot. Deciding she, and not the visual harassers, owned her body, Paula created the world's first pair of pantyhose. Because no one knew how to make something that hadn't been invented yet, Bunyan broke with femynist principles on this occasion and sewed the garment herself, dubbing it a "sexual harassment suit of armor."

Getting a leg up on the womyn's lefts movement, she later dispensed with dresses altogether, and wore jeans like all the johns. In another pointed political statement, she stopped wearing her chest shackle, and persuaded Lucy the Bovine Companion to do the same. Paula's "brassieres" had been fashioned from canvas coverings for trained traveling animal prisoners, or circus tents, and she sometimes used them to smother brush fires. One night, in a symbolic act of protest, she held a size 4,400D chest shackle above the trees and burned it, illuminating a tri-state area and unintentionally igniting a forest fire.

Undaunted, Paula doused the blaze by uprooting a fallen spruce, hollowing it out with a fingernail, sucking the water of an entire tributary into her mouth (while gently dropping into a fishpond the schools of trout she inadvertently trapped), and spewing the water onto the flames from high above the tree line. Sadly, Bunyan didn't see that woodland conflagrations are Nature's way of purging and replenishing its forests.

The arrival of mechanical saws sparked a crisis in the lumberjane community. Workplace automation made many unskilled loggers suddenly explore unexpected career paths. Some of these displaced laborers complained about the unfair advantage Paula Bunyan's size and strength provided her in a suddenly more competitive global marketplace. Worse than the impact on people, however, was the effect on botanical citizens: Mechanical saws slayed trees at a much faster rate. From her perch above the woods, Paula watched long lines of animal refugees in flight from ever-growing swaths of felled forest. Mechanization seemed to have just one benefit. As with substitution of the electric chair for the noose, replacement of axes with power saws afforded tree victims a swifter, more merciful end.

To save the jobs of the remaining lumberjanes, Paula had to prove the superiority of humyn workers. In a famous showdown of myn against machine, she pitted herself and Babe the Blue Ox against a fully automated sawmill. Starting with equal piles of tree carcasses, the two sides raced to see which could more quickly cut and stack the deceased timber.

The face-off was delayed until animal lefts demonstrators won a pledge of designated work breaks and accrued comp time for the Blue Ox. Then, once the contest began, Babe's unmatched strength won out as she gracefully hauled lumber much more quickly than the factory's clattering conveyor belt. At the same time, the blade of Paula's giant ax glowed red-hot from nonstop chopping, and sliced through logs like Lorena Bobbitt through fat-free oleomargarine. Bunyan's coworkers, who had once hooted and whistled after her bod, now filled the factory with cheers for her undeniable professional competence.

As Paula raised her ax to split the final chunk of tree carcass, the mechanical sawmill had fallen hopelessly behind. Bunyan triumphantly swung the tool into the tree flesh— and cried out as her hands were wracked with pain and her giant blade, flying off the handle, felled an entire wall of the factory. Both of Paula's wrists were sprained, and her massive shoulder muscles were wracked by excruciating spasms. In horror she inspected the log, and discovered that an eco-warrior, to protest the continued assassination of trees, had placed a stainless-steel spike under the bark. A painful but valuable lesson had been dealt to the free-swinging roughneck.

Paula and the Blue Ox could do nothing but watch the mechanical saw cut its way unopposed through the final stacks of wood. Injured and bummed, the lumberjane crept out of the mill past the dumbfounded spectators. She took extended sick leave and filed a personal injury suit.

Afforded the time to reflect upon the growing plight of the forest citizens, Paula Bunyan was radicalized. Upon returning to her job she organized work slowdowns that forced the timber companies to accept a "plant closure" act, whereby squirrels, woodpeckers, and termites residing in trees and other large plants slated for destruction were informed in advance. (To maintain profit margins, the companies refused to pay the relocation costs of the displaced creatures.) Few temporary workers* were willing to cross the picket line when they saw Bunyan's strapping, 120-meter form, with her mainsail-sized protest sign ominously blotting out the sun.

During union meetings of the idled loggers, Paula convinced everyone to stop wearing spiked shoes when shimmying up a trunk, thus ending the widespread torture of bark. A newfound respect for the ecology swept the timber industry. At groceries throughout the Pacific Northwest, customers refused brown paper bags in favor of reusable cloth sacks.

Paula Bunyan's relentless agitation forced the faceless

---

* Scabs.

logging companies to designate all their forest properties as protected land.* A minor side effect was a noticeable corporate downsizing, as all the lumberjanes lost their jobs. After their cruel but well-paying employment, ex-loggers were reduced to flipping flapjanes for pennies an hour.

When the shutdown of the Oregon logging industry was complete, the legendary Bunyan retired to her home state of Maine, and founded the movement to place a refundable five-cent deposit on that state's soda bottles. She saved billions of additional trees by pressuring Publishers Clearing House to cut in half the notices stuffed into its sweepstakes envelopes. She considered a job as a political pamphleteer, but the sharply rising cost of paper from logging restrictions had sent the publishing industry into a tailspin, rendering unviable such a career option. In her last public campaign, Paula Bunyan futilely lobbied the custodians of Mount Rushmore to carve an image of Sex Object the Blue Ox onto their all-male mountain sculpture.

---

* "Preserves," which can refer to the boiled extracts of defenseless crushed fruit, should be avoided.

The Illicit Weapons Discharge at the Fairly Pleasant Detention Center for Hooved Animal Companions*

Tombstone, Arizona, was torn in the 1880s by a struggle between two feuding factions, the Clantons and the Earps, who had somewhat varying

---

* Shoot-out at the O.K. Corral.

perspectives on crime and social justice. Ike Clanton headed a social club, or gang, for misunderstood members of the outlaw community. Ike's civic group included his sibling Bill, the Tom and Frank McLowery siblings, and hired gunperson Bill Claiborne, who was touted as another "Billy the Goat," that is, Billy the Kid. (It is speciesocentric to presume "kid" means a child instead of a youthful goat.) The Clantons were often joined by gunslinger John Ringo, who was a mediocre drummer but a skilled *pistolero*.

In idle moments, Ike Clanton fancied himself head of a freedom-loving private militia battling the oppression of federal marshals. Meanwhile, his grassroots community organization offered its violence-susceptible members the sort of dependable, loving support group that mainstream society wouldn't provide. Their social adjustment problems indicate the Clantons hadn't been raised in a caring orphanage or placed in a nurturing Head Start program.

Like many clubs today, Ike and his bunch wore "gang colors." Their repressive culture, which insisted on making arbitrary moral distinctions between "good guys" and "bad guys," compounded its error with tintism, linking clothing of color with "outlaws" and pale clothing of noncolor with the enforcement authorities, as in expressions like "The sheriff and posse were the myn in white hats."

The Clantons were the Robbing Hoods of the "Untamed West."* In their romyntic pose of cattle rustlers, desperado

---

* Wild West. "Wild" is a derogatory word for nonhumyn animals in their natural state, as it implies they are "savage" and somehow less civilized than humyn animals. The word "untamed" gives a more accurate sense of the proud mental state of undomesticated creatures.

associations saved herds of cattle from death marches to Kansas holding pens and eventual transfer to Chicago slaughterhouses. Aside from striking a blow for freedom, their "livestock liberations" forced formerly flesh-eating ranchers onto a benign diet of vegetarian chili. Clubs like the Clantons were disgusted by cowpersons who would nearly strangle horses by lassoing them, destroy their spirit by "breaking" them, and scar their hides with brands.

By holding up stagecoaches and shaking down sod-busters, rugged individualists such as Ike Clanton expropriated the mineral and vegetable wealth drained from Northeast Mexico, or "the Southwest," as gringos who stole the region from Mexico call it. By derailing locomotives, they blunted the exploitation of Chinese and Irish laborers who laid down and repaired the region's railways. They slowed the culture shock of exposing preindustrial native cultures to advanced, "Iron Horse" technology. Despite the many and predictable train mishaps, the government never required passenger air bags on sleeper cars and cabooses.

News of the Clantons' exploits spread by telegraph lines laid across country and ocean without careful study of the possibly harmful effect of electrical currents on humyn, fish, and insect communities. Many locales in the Northeast Mexico of the Untamed West shunned revenue from nonexploitative industries like tourism, a sustainable option the herstoric town of Tombstone follows today.

While the Clanton club embodied the free-spirited criminal community's legitimate rage at unjust social conditions, the Earp siblings personified the stifling authori-

tarianism of Tombstone's ruling class. The three marshals
were called Wyatt, Morgan, and Virgil, the latter named
for a Roman propagandist formerly studied in colleges
that force-fed students reading lists of so-called "Great
Books." The Earps' henchperson was John "Doc"
Holliday. Despite his medical background, Holliday
shunned holistic medicine and low-cost herbal treatments
in favor of expensive new health technologies like antisep-
tics, X rays, and anesthesia.

All the Earps were two meters short, fat-disadvantaged,
and sported Stetdaughter hats. Drooping phallically from
their hips were six-shot Youthful Equestrian Companion
(Colt) revolvers, whose handles were inlaid with pearls
borrowed without their oyster owners' permission. The
Earps had been deputized without first undergoing rigor-
ous training programs in police-community relations, use
of nonlethal force, and the psychology of the stagecoach
robber.

The town of Tombstone encouraged the oddball notion
that private citizens had a role in fighting the law-averse,
and refused to see that crime was almost entirely the result
of weak gun control. In the Untamed West, "law-abiding"
residents, and not just social club members, were permitted to own deadly weapons. There was even a "hidden gun
law" by which a hotel's sex entrepreneur* could legally
keep a pistol at the ready in her ankle holster. Tombstone
failed to buy back the Clantons' guns with cash awards
and a promise not to prosecute for prior gun possession.

---

* Prostitute.

The town's rehabilitation center was a fortress of shotguns, jail cells, and bristling rifle racks, with nary a can of Mace or a box of dumdum bullets. Detainees were denied weightlifting equipment and cable TV.

The Earps were backed by Tombstone's Law and Order League, a self-appointed citizens group that put "victims' rights" ahead of the overlooked concerns of equestrian appropriators (horse thieves), transnational freedom fighters (*banditos*), and hired gunpersons. The League failed to address the underlying social causes of law adversity with redeye addiction treatment programs and supervised games of midnight lassoing.

October 26, 1881, witnessed the Illicit Weapons Discharge at the Fairly Pleasant Detention Center for Hooved Animal Companions. The Clanton club rode into town and gently tied their beloved animal friends to a rounded, horizontal slab of tree carcass outside the public place for illicit beverage and tobacco consumption. Upon learning the marshals were in Tombstone, Ike Clanton uttered his famous remark, "The Earps gotta leave—this town ain't space-endowed enough for the both of us." Clanton's advice, if followed, would have peaceably resolved the intergroup conflict.

Later that tragic day, Virgil Earp confronted Ike Clanton outside the saloon. When Clanton raised his rifle in response, Earp knocked it aside and hit Clanton in the head with his pistol derriere.* Earp, who adhered to an

---

* Pistol butt. Many find the word "butt" offensive, for it represents the remains of the most widely consumed nicotine product.

inflexible "one strike, you're out" rule of law enforcement, hauled Clanton before the town judge. Instead of censuring the marshal, the misguided magistrate fined the social club president for disturbing the peace.

At this hearing, Virgil Earp didn't prove that Ike Clanton raised his rifle with malicious intent. Earp couldn't even have been certain, beyond a reasonable doubt, that the rifle was loaded. The other club members in attendance hadn't drawn their self-defense tools at Virgil's provocation, but had shown remarkable restraint after Virgil threatened to blow their heads off. Instead of trying to establish a dialogue with Clanton, Earp—without calling out for backup—had hit him with a dangerous object, which might have gone off by mistake, possibly injuring an innocent, person-slaughtering club member, or worse, an equestrian comrade sipping placidly at the saloon's water trough.

After the pistol-whipping incident, the Earps provocatively stocked up on weapons at the town gun shop. With the Earps' apparent support, Tombstone had no waiting period for the purchase of derringers by deputized marshals facing mortal danger. Virgil Earp borrowed a shotgun from the Wells Fargo office, a notorious delivery firm whose frenetic schedule pushed the hooved animal companions of its riders beyond nonhumyn endurance. Making a mockery of his Hippocratic oath, the hypocritical Holliday accepted Virgil's shotgun. The arms buildup convinced the Clantons a diplomatic solution was urgent, for they invited their tormentors out to a round of mediation at the Fairly Pleasant Detention Center.

At midafternoon Doc Holliday and the three heavily armed Earp siblings strutted across town to the equine prison. The Earps had to walk because, like most settlements in the Sunbelt, Tombstone had underinvested in public transit. When the four gun enthusiasts arrived at their destination, five members of the Clanton social club were interfacing nonbelligerently next to the equine holding cell, or stable. Two innocent, four-legged bystanders were lolling next to them.

The Earp siblings left Holliday and his shotgun at the detention center's entrance, probably to prevent unbiased observers from witnessing what ensued. Their loaded pistols in plain view, the Earps came to a halt just a few menacing steps from the Clantons. Despite the risk of imminent hostilities, and their responsibility as law officers, the Earps did not move the animal companions to safety. Ike Clanton, according to an unconfirmed account, made a heartfelt plea on their behalf: "Hey, it's awful enough they've lost their freedom, and that we're about to trash their home. So let's at least shoo them out of harm's way."

But Virgil Earp turned an auditorily inconvenienced ear to Clanton. He abruptly answered: "Put up any limbs you may have. You're all under arrest!"

The available facts condemn the Earps in what is known as "the Fairly Pleasant Detention Center Massacre."

After Virgil's intemperate, unconditional demand, gunfire broke out. A bullet sent club member Frank McLowery to the dust while his sibling Tom, bravely refusing to fire, took refuge behind a horse. Wyatt Earp did not walk the unfortunate creature aside, but cravenly fired while she was still blocking his view, lodging a bullet in her derriere. Doc Holliday riddled brave Tom with blasts from the shotgun, which he then threw to the ground, possibly in despair over his cruel act, more likely because he was out of bullets. Billy Clanton fell down wounded, and was shot again while *still on the ground.* Two club members fled; although ballistic tests were inexplicably never conducted, it is almost certain they didn't fire their guns.

Ike Clanton never discharged his instrument of self-defense. He tried to give himself up, shouting: "Don't leave me biologically challenged*—I ain't shooting!"

Yet Wyatt Earp, in violation of standard procedure, refused to take him into protective custody. Wyatt callously replied, "Get to fighting or get out of here," and Ike got out, escaping with Billy "the Goat" Claiborne by way of the equestrian residence.

Afterward, the Earps claimed their foes had drawn first, but it was they who had police artists sketch pictures of the escaped club members. As for the claim the Clantons fired their guns first, no daguerreotype or video camera was on hand to record what really happened.

A strong indication of who was really to blame is the Clantons' higher casualties. Three club members were biologically altered with cured cattle flesh attached to their lower extremities—that is, they died with their boots on. Sadly, their burial plots at Boot Hill graveyard outside town took away valuable space from a fragile desert

---

* "Don't kill me!"

ecosystem. Their bodies should have been laid out in the open where environmentally conscious wolves and mountain lions could have quickly recycled them.

In contrast to the Clantons' heavy losses, Virgil and Morgan Earp were only wounded, and Doc Holliday suffered a nick in the posterior, a fitting injury considering the grievous hurt inflicted on the horse's keister, an injury the callous doctor never treated. The injured critter anguished over the absence of organ donor cards for animals. Holliday also ignored the second equine, who undoubtedly suffered from shock and gunsmoke inhalation. Indeed, clouds of smoke billowed up from the weapons' discharge, and mixed with the soot of mesquite barbecues to foul Tombstone's pristine preindustrial air, which was marred only by the ever-present smell of disease-hosting horse droppings outside every home and public place.

Misconduct charges were never filed against the Earps, even though none served the Clantons warrants or let them cable their defense attorneys. The surviving Clantons never filed suit against the Colt and Remington companies for making the arms the Earps wielded with such devastating effect. Finally, the hooved animal companions at the Fairly Pleasant Detention Center weren't compensated for damage to their persons or lodgings or shattered mental states.

Theodore Roosevelt, the Bullock Moose

The most regrettable episode in Theodore Roosevelt's life was his leadership of the "Rough Exploiters of Equestrian Slaves," or Rough Riders, during the 1898 Act of American Aggression Against Spain. During this military stint, which the forty-year-old Roosevelt used to surmount a midlife crisis, he hung with persons of diverse backgrounds but for a wrongful cause. He officered a regiment of Cherokee Indigenous Persons, persons of color, and western cowpersons. The multicultural unit also contained affluent Princeton and Yale students who actually volunteered to fight instead of staging university teach-ins against U.S. imperialism. Unlike many politicians, Roosevelt eagerly served his country when he should have sidestepped the war machine through a college deferment or claim of personal injury.

The Rough Exploiters of Equestrian Slaves departed for Cuba from Tampa, Florida*—a formerly Latina region stolen by Anglo-Americans. Due to a lack of transport, most of the horses were left behind, fortunately sparing them the risk of combat, and forcing the soldiers to risk Courage-Averse (Yellow) Fever by slogging through Cuba's wetlands in midsummer heat.

The Rough Exploiters seized San Juan Hill with a unit of blacks, who disgracefully took part in the Yankee power grab instead of switching sides and fighting with their class-struggle allies. Meanwhile, the U.S. navy sank a Spanish fleet at Santiago harbor, miring thousands of birds and maritime denizens in a massive oil spill.

The Act of American Aggression Against Spain made Cuba an American colony until its liberation by Fidel Castro. Before Fidel modernized the economy with exports of displaced persons and under-the-counter pharmaceuticals, Cuba produced only one thing of value:

---

* Tampa's sister city is Leningrad, recently renamed "St. Petersburg" by reactionary elements.

thickly rolled cancer sticks for yuppies intent on flaunting conspicuous consumption.

Teddy Roosevelt's biological father was a successful banker who assuaged his guilt at moneymaking with philanthropy. His birthmother was Martha Bullock ("Bullock," incidentally, means a bobbittized or castrated bull who got exactly what he deserved). Although he grew into a vigorous outdoorsmyn, Roosevelt was a weak, asthmatic child. His nonfoster dad took him on fast carriage rides to force air into his weak lungs, mistreating the horses by whipping them into a gallop, and putting at risk Teddy, who rode without a child's restraining seat.

Birthed in 1858, Theodore Roosevelt was distantly related to Franklin Delano Roosevelt. FDR was president during the Condition of Being Very Emotionally Challenged, when the depressed economy was in a meaningful downturn. He battled underemployment with public works like the Grand Asian-Laborer (Coulee) Dam, the construction of which may have drowned thousands of snail darters. Franklin Roosevelt set up an "alphabet soup" of federal agencies like the WPA, the FDIC, and—to combat the ill effects of lifting Prohibition—AA. Hard times ended with his National Recovery Administration, or NRA, whose advocacy of job-creating gun production was fulfilled by the full-employment economy of the wartime 1940s.

Teddy Roosevelt enrolled at Harvard in 1876, the centennial year of Turtle Island's formal occupation by the United States. He was an overachieving student who authored the first of his thirty-eight processed tree carcasses and kept a habit of reading a carcass a day. A believer in the illusion of free will, he felt he could improve his health by vigorous running and weightlifting, and brawled his way into the Harvard boxing program's title bout. The lesson was clear: TR should have shunned pugilism and started a movement to abolish the vicious sport.

After a period of sexual harassment the Victorian era termed "courting," Roosevelt married a person of the opposite gender. Their 1880 wedding was in a Massachusetts village that was later hometown to Michael Dukakis, a presidential nominee who exhibited machismo comparable to Teddy Roosevelt's by posing in an Army tank during a campaign commercial. After their domestic incarceration ceremony, the newlyweds boarded a steamship to spend their introduction to legalized rape in Europe.

After the unexpected interment of his first domestic partner, a widowed Roosevelt sought refuge running a Dakota Goodlands* cattle prison camp called the Chimney Butte or, less coarsely, the Chimney Derriere. TR fell victim to auditory discrimination by rugged cowpersons who lampooned the odd-sounding voice of the refined, educated Easterner. In reaction, Roosevelt conformed to peer group expectations, personally halting attempted escapes by stampeding herds, even though his Republican political party had once supported the Underground Subway† for escaping human slaves.

---

* Dakota Badlands. "Bad" is a subjective value judgment.
† Underground Railroad. To encourage use of mass transit, the term subway is preferred.

Far from introducing endangered species into the surrounding countryside, Teddy Roosevelt hunted down cougars trying to restore the balance of Nature among his swollen sheep and cattle herds. After years of atrocities, a record blizzard that seemed to offer clear evidence of planetary warming froze most of the steers on the Goodlands ranch, ending their misery and Roosevelt's tyranny.

Later in life, a globe-trotting Roosevelt went on killing sprees in East Africa, and displayed stuffed trophies of mayhem on the walls of his Sagamore Hill home. He once shot an enraged charging bear instead of lying facedown and staying very, very still. In Brazil, he explored the sources of the Amazon, named for a proud band of womyn warriors who blocked oppressors like Hercules from their military units because of inferior physical strength.

As president, Roosevelt atoned for his environmental misdeeds by founding many national parks, and even barred fast-food restaurants from their grounds. He quashed an attempt by radical Republicans to privatize Yellowstone Park and give bottling companies the water rights to Old Faithful. His refusal, during a presidential hunting trip, to gun down a bear cub sparked a nationwide "Teddy bear" craze in which thousands of preadults patronized the imaginary representatives of a noble species.

Roosevelt's first appointive post was to head the U.S. civil service, where he insisted on picking government workers by merit alone, instead of allocating top slots along ethnic, gender, gender-preference, income, national-ity, territorial, religious, political, nepotistic, fund-raising, and buddy-buddy lines. The civil service tests Roosevelt established for the U.S. government were flatly biased: The exams were in English, and the questions presumed a knowledge of the U.S. government. Teddy Roosevelt reformed the Postal Service, and the absence of postal office shootings on his watch shows he closed this vital outlet for venting worker rage.

A biography of TR provides a psychoanalysis of his stint as assistant secretary of the Navy:

> *Roosevelt stressed his war-mongering maxim, "Speak softly and carry a size-advantaged sliver of tree carcass." He poured his repressed phallobellicosity into battleship funding that would have been better spent on kindergarten condom distributions. Roosevelt also suffered from the delusion that placing sailwomyn aboard fighting ships during lengthy voyages in close quarters would lead, at least initially, to multiple pregnancies and a corresponding decrease in fighting prowess.*

Hailed as a war criminal* upon his return from leading the Rough Exploiters of Equestrian Slaves, Roosevelt was elected governor of the state of Manhattan (the original, native name for New York). Touted for still-higher office, he issued a misstatement echoed by many politicos since: "I am more than content to be governor, and shall not care if I ever hold another office." The following year, TR

---

* War hero.

accepted the Republican nomination for vice president, although golf was one of the few sports he didn't play.

He and President William McKinley handily defeated William Jennings Bryan, who ran for and lost the presidency even more often than Lyndon LaRouche. After his retirement from the job of perpetual campaigner, the Democrat Bryan defended the fundamentalist religious position in the Scopes "monkey trial," which indicates he was in the wrong political party, and explains why he lost so many elections.

In 1901, one year after turn-of-the-century jubilees staged by adherents of the B.C.-A.D. convention for classifying time, President McKinley was removed from office in a nonpeaceful manner by an emotionally challenged anarchist. (An anarchist is a person who believes, like a Republican, that there should be no government. A Democrat is a person who believes in government by anarchy.) Within two months, the assassin was arrested, tried, and executed; needless to say, Johnnie Cochran was not on his legal defense team. After President McKinley's demise, Teddy Roosevelt became Sachem Executive.*

Long before the civil rights era, Theodore Roosevelt was deeply involved in race relations. He was the first president to invite a melanin-endowed myn to the Melanin-Deprived House for dinner. In foreign affairs, he signed a "Gentleperson's Agreement" with Tokyo to limit the number of immigrants then filling up California's schools. Like

---

* Chief Executive. Sachem is the Native American name for "chief," a term that may offend Jimmy Olsen's editor. Sachem Executive is a suggested substitute for "Great Melanin-Deprived Parent" (Great White Father).

recent admissions quotas on Chinese and Vietnamese students, the agreement spared native-born scholars the stress of competing in math and science subjects where Asian newcomers have an inherently unfair advantage.

President Roosevelt was nicknamed the "trust buster"— not for broken campaign promises but for breaking up monopolies under the Shermyn Antitrust Act. By forcing greater competition, better quality, and lower prices, he permitted the beef and oil industries to afflict even more customers with their unhealthful products. An advocate of the "Square Deal" for the working humyn, he forced a strike-ravaged coal industry to raise wages, but failed to enact a strike-avoiding salary cap for the players of the deceased ball era. He reduced the work week for female and child laborers, thus crimping their wages and ability to leave domestic imprisonment. The sheer number of Roosevelt's accomplishments was amazing because, like any elected politician, he had to spend 98 percent of his time raising campaign funds.

Believing persons should master Nature, not nurture it, Roosevelt sponsored the Panama Canal. Its construction, while cutting travel time between Marin County and Manhattan, wrecked delicate coastal ecologies by mixing the waters of two previously separate oceans. The Canal's huge gash across the Panamanian landscape severed the south-north migration patterns of many land animals. In a visit to the Canal Zone, the Bullock Moose became the first president to travel outside the country: The Zone provided a stunning backdrop for photo ops to boost the president's poll numbers.

After leaving politics for four years, TR returned as standard bearer for the Bullock Moose party. He would have been the first ex-president to regain office since Grover Cleveland, a fatism survivor whose portly shape inspired the term Oval Office, and who abjectly failed his twelve-step Eaters Anonymous program. The only other president to win back his job was Jimmy Carter, a Georgian grower of legumes high in saturated fat whose diplomatic missions in the 1990s effectively made him president a second time.

Misjudged Nazis Defend Their "Unique Culture": An Alternate View of the Second World War

Most accounts of the Second World War are vastly oversimplified. The conflict is usually described as an attempt by "jackbooted, Nazi-helmeted thugs" to take over the earth. Value judgments are notoriously subjective, however, and the truth, as always, is somewhere in the middle. In fact, the much-maligned Nazis and their Imperial Japanese friends were struggling to preserve their distinct way of life against an encroaching hegemony of Western imperialists.

Only a cultural bigot would deny the Nazis made many positive contributions. They invented a Volkswagen "people's car" that was remarkably fuel-efficient. During the widespread underemployment of the 1930s, they created jobs with public works like the forts of the Siegfried Line. They founded the Autobahn, a society dedicated to the preservation of birds. As a blockaded, resource-deprived country, Nazi Germany devised synthetic fuels which could prove invaluable during the next energy crisis.

The Nazis' V-2 rocket, although causing collateral damage in London and other towns, symbolized an understandable drive for technological independence. Further, this wonder weapon was the precursor of orbital boosters that immigrant Nazi scientists fleeing harsh persecution in Europe built for the U.S. space program. The Apollo moonshots were only possible, therefore, through the German Motherland's wise investment in far-ranging scientific research.

Progressive Nazis supported banning offensive language on college campuses, and enforced their point of view with spirited book burnings. "Racially insensitive" professors were shunted aside in a forward-looking system of preferential firing. In its enthusiastic support of euthanasia, the Nazi party anticipated the assisted suicide movement, whereby angels of mercy libeled as "doctors of death" help those deemed unfit for further life reach a comfortable end. Firm believers in government-financed art, fascists staged pagan pageants that gloried in an ideal Teutonic past where forest-dwelling tribes of Vandals and Visigoths dwelt in perfect harmony with Nature.

The full name of the Nazi party, the National Socialist Workers Party, shows it was at heart a progressive, pro-labor movement. In fact, for a time the Nazis formed a mutual defense pact with Soviet Russia, which by the 1930s had also blossomed into an occupational, civil liberties, and environmental paradise. The construction by Communist elder statesperson "Uncle Joe" Stalin of extensive reeducation centers faithfully followed deeply rooted Russian traditions stretching back to Czar Ivan the Less Than Satisfactory.* Stalin, who had a troubled childhood, should be absolved of guilt for the twenty million or so scholars who terminated their studies before graduating from his reeducation facilities.

The charismatic leader of the embattled Nazi community was "Dolph" Hitler, to use the first-name informality now customary for referring to political leaders. Early in his public-service career, Dolph was arrested after attempting an armed seizure of power from a Munich beer hall. He should be forgiven for this, for German culture is notoriously tolerant toward the consumption of high-caloric, alcohol-laden beverages. After the failed *putsch*, Hitler

---

* Ivan the Terrible. "Terrible" is a value judgment.

served a brief prison term under a compassionate early-release program which rehabilitated a large percentage of its megalomaniac inmate population.

Der Führer was a gifted but commercially nonviable landscape painter denied a societally sanctioned outlet for his creative energies. He had the moody, sometimes irascible temperament of the bohemian artist; indeed, he may have occupied Bohemia and the rest of Czechoslovakia out of sheer affinity for its culture. Something of a New Age mystic, Hitler was a strict vegetarian who retained an astrologer to confirm his self-proclaimed role as a Man of Destiny. Forward-looking on family issues, he entered into a childless, common-law marriage with Significant Other Eva Braun. His personal habits compare favorably with those of rival British leader Winston Churchill. The latter drank heavily, ate red meats and blood puddings, and smoked cigars. It hardly seems accidental his first name was *Winston,* and that he was descended from British imperialist the Duke of *Marlboro.*

Hitler's life was not without controversy. In his youthful role of street demagogue, he urged the restoration of German power "by any means necessary." At times insensitive to others' feelings, he characterized blacks as subhuman, "brown-eyed devils." From his cultural perspective, non-Nordics were engaged in a vast conspiracy against the German people. Like Napoleon, Alexander the Great, and other vertically challenged leaders, Hitler was a heightism survivor who took out frustration over a lack of stature by trying to conquer the world.

If Dolph Hitler had lived for the Nuremberg war crimes

trials, he might have been acquitted of the primary charge of ethnic cleansing. After all, the Nazi leader suffered from a mild testosterone deficiency* that contributed to pronounced mood swings and periods of temporary insanity. Such speculation is moot, however, because Hitler expired at the end of the Second World War. Many knowledgeable conspiracy theorists believe elements of the U.S. government, including the Army, Air Force, and Navy, played a key role in his premature demise. Some modern-day skinhead and militia groups sympathetic to Hitler's viewpoint believe a swat team from the Justice Department's ATF agency was also involved.

The United States entered the Second World War after Japan's stealthy, well-coordinated act of self-defense at Pearl Harbor. Imperial Japan was defending itself from a pattern of U.S. intimidation dating from Commodore Matthew Perry's forced 1850s opening of Japanese ports and extending past George Bush's 1992 regurgitation of sushi at a Tokyo state banquet. The United States precipitated the Pearl Harbor tragedy by cutting off Japan's petroleum supply, a hostile act which nonetheless reduced smog in Nippon's congested cities. The American government has never formally apologized for starting the war.

The slanted U.S. view of Imperial Japan's behavior focuses on its alleged abuse of civilians and prisoners-of-war. For example, after billeting troops in the Philippines, the Japanese accompanied their American guests on "the Bataan High-Mortality Promenade," renamed "the

---

* A missing testicle.

Bataan Death March" by revisionist U.S. scholars. In Korea, native "comfort ladies" were politely asked at gunpoint to share their quarters with General Tojo's soldiers. Japanese troops on leave in China busied themselves with "the Involuntary Acquisition of Nanking" ("the Rape of Nanking"), during which several hundred thousand Chinese civilians were reclassified as missing in action.

Tokyo defended its unique indigenous culture in outlying provinces such as Singapore, Burma, and Guam. In these locales, Japanese Imperial forces freed colonial peoples from imperialist oppressors by setting up indigenous governments, mislabeled "puppet regimes" by subjective observers. Meanwhile, all over the western Pacific, high-tech, state-of-the-art firms such as Mitsubishi launched headline-grabbing promotional campaigns for quality exports like the "Zero" fighter plane.

In nonpeaceful encounters on Pacific isles such as Guadalcanal, charging Imperial troops would shout "*Bonsai!*"—a tribute to the very size-disadvantaged Japanese plants that consume few water and soil resources. When the U.S. navy intruded upon their home islands, Nippon's pilots signaled their support, through *kamikaze* attacks on enemy ships, for the right to choose one's time of death with dignity.

In fairness to the United States it should be noted that massive U.S. air raids on Japanese population centers like Tokyo, and German ones like Dresden, led to some unavoidable casualties, as they employed imprecise, nonsurgical ordnance to effect collateral damage on civilian assets. And the Americans, despite a critical wartime shortage of housing, went out of their way to build guest hostels for the entire Japanese-American population of the West Coast.

The start of the war in Europe also cries out for a fair and accurate reinterpretation. In 1939, the League of Nations—the predecessor of the United Nations—temporarily suspended its mediation efforts in Eastern Europe after Dolph Hitler and Uncle Joe Stalin acquired portions of Poland without first seeking Poland's formal permission. Britain and France then started a global holocaust by declaring war.

Instead of taking this provocative step, the Western powers should have petitioned the League of Nations, in the manner of today's UN, to facilitate a regional peace process. Like the UN in Bosnia, for example, the League could have urged splitting Poland into autonomous ethnic enclaves. The Nazis could have administered the western part of Poland, the Soviets the eastern part, and the Poles, Jews, and other parties to the negotiations whatever territory was left. Neville Chamberlain, the British proponent of diplomatic fair play,* would have been an ideal choice to head up a peacekeeping force.

Decisive military action by the League's forces could have been endlessly debated, but never seriously considered. League air attacks could have been forever threatened, but seldom executed, against Nazi airplanes and artillery targeting defenseless Polish cities. Whenever attackers leveled the downtowns of "safe havens," a League bomber could have dropped a dud onto an

---

* Appeasement.

advancing tank. As a less violent alternative, diplomats could have placed intimidating, baton-wielding peacekeepers between Polish towns and Nazi panzer divisions. If a town was surrounded by advancing fighters, the peacekeepers could have evacuated the population, making the conflict's regrettably haphazard massacres more predictable and easily administered. As in Bosnia, for instance, the presence of blue-helmeted peacekeepers in Poland would have prevented more forceful intervention to stem the bloodshed, lest such involvement endanger the peacekeepers. Peace would have been at hand.

Despite self-righteous condemnation of the supposed ethical lapses of Dolph Hitler and General Tojo, the United States ignored its own leaders' grievous misbehavior. General George Patton, after a widely publicized incident in which he slapped one of his own soldiers, was unaccountably retained after martial skills were judged more important than personal peccadilloes. General Douglas MacArthur was not reprimanded, by a surgeon general or anyone else, for his brazen public display and implicit endorsement of a corncob pipe. President Franklin Roosevelt never released all medical records relating to his polio, nor did he resign over his refusal of full disclosure. To beat the Nazis to the atomic bomb, Roosevelt pushed the Manhattan Project when he should have filed a friend-of-the-court suit with antinuke activists to block the development of nuclear arms. The press covered up General Dwight Eisenhower's steamy affair with his Army driver, permitting him to execute the D day invasion. Instead of being grateful to the media, Eisenhower may have borne a grudge, for he forbade live coverage of the Normandy landings, even though the networks would have agreed to a one-hour delay in broadcasting information about Allied troop movements. Time and again, expediency overwhelmed principle.

Probably the most important lesson of the Second World War* is that one must always label an important event by its proper, inoffensive name. The conclusion of the conflict in the Pacific should be termed V-P (Victory in the Pacific) Day. The archaic term V-J Day, for Victory over Japan, deeply offends the sensibilities of surviving organizers of the Bataan High-Mortality Promenade. The end of the disagreement in Europe has always been thoughtfully termed V-E (Victory in Europe) Day because there were two defeated European powers, Dolph Hitler's Germany and Benny Mussolini's Italy. The term V-G (Victory over Germany) Day would have hurt the feelings of surviving Nazis.

---

* Some consider the term Second World War inaccurate because most combat from 1939 to 1945 occurred between the affluent Eurocentric or industrialized peoples of the Northern Hemisphere. Many emerging nations in the Southern Hemisphere stayed peacefully on the sidelines. A suggested substitute term is the "Second Northern Hemispheric Disagreement." The harsh-sounding word "War" may also offend, and can be replaced by a milder term such as "Disagreement," "Dispute Resolution," or "Nonpeaceful Diplomacy."

Biographical Index